Who Defends America?

Race, Sex, and Class in the Armed Forces

Les Aspin

McGeorge Bundy

Cynthia H. Enloe

Robert K. Fullinwider

Lawrence J. Korb

Elsie Moore

Charles C. Moskos

Alvin J. Schexnider

A. Wade Smith

Roger Wilkins

Edited by Edwin Dorn

Joint Center for Political Studies Press
Washington, D.C.

The Joint Center for Political Studies is a national nonprofit institution that conducts research on public policy issues of special concern to black Americans and promotes informed and effective involvement of blacks in the governmental process. Founded in 1970, the Joint Center provides independent and nonpartisan analyses through research, publication, and outreach programs.

We gratefully acknowledge the support of the Johnson Foundation, the Ford Foundation, and the Rockefeller Foundation.

Distributed by arrangement with
University Press of America, Inc.
4720 Boston Way
Lanham, MD 20706

3 Henrietta Street
London WC2E 8LU England

British Cataloging in Publication Information Available

Library of Congress Cataloging-in-Publication Data

Who defends America? : race, sex, and class in the armed forces / edited by Edwin Dorn.
p.   cm.
1. United States– –Armed Forces– –Afro–Americans. 2. United States–
–Armed Forces– –Women. 3. Sociology, Military– –United States– –History
– –20th century. 4. Manpower– –United States. I. Dorn, Edwin.
UB418.A47W48   1989   89–1712 CIP
355'.008996073– –dc19
ISBN 0–941410–77–3 (alk. paper)
ISBN 0–941410–78–1 (pbk. : alk. paper)

CONTENTS

LIST OF TABLES

LIST OF FIGURES

FOREWORD

W*ho Defends America? Race, Sex, and Class in the Armed Forces,* explores the increasingly significant role of blacks in the nation's armed services. Blacks are 12 percent of the U.S. population but 20 percent of all active duty military personnel and about 30 percent of the army's soldiers. Should these statistics bother us? Is there something wrong with relying heavily on one racial or ethnic group to defend the nation? How do we weigh the benefits that young black men and women derive from military service against the heavy burdens they would bear if the nation were to become engaged in a major conventional war?

It is difficult to address those questions without some background on broader national security issues. What are our nation's strategic interests, who threatens them, and how is the nation preparing to respond? The first three chapters contain the policy perspectives needed to make sense of the specific questions about blacks in the military, that the authors of the remaining chapters then go on to address.

This volume first began to take shape during a symposium held at the Johnson Foundation Wingspread Conference Center in Racine, Wisconsin, in June 1982. The meeting provided a rare opportunity for scholars, current and former public officials, and representatives of major civil rights organizations to discuss national defense. The several chapters of this study, some of which have been updated, reflect the variety of perspectives and styles of thought that one would expect from such a diverse and talented group.

The Joint Center is grateful to the various authors whose views are contained in this volume. We also appreciate the encouragement we received from Dr. William Boyd, President Emeritus of the Johnson Foundation, which co-sponsored the 1982 meeting, and from Enid Schoettle of the Ford Foundation, which supports the Joint Center's clearinghouse on military affairs. In addition, funds from the Rockefeller Foundation were used to support the symposium.

We wish to thank Martin Binkin of the Brookings Institution, Robert Hill of the Bureau of Social Science Research, and John Butler, professor of sociology at the University of Texas, for reviewing the manuscript and offering a number of helpful suggestions.

We are grateful to the many people who helped produce this book. Frank Dexter Brown, Catherine Iino, Mark DeFrancis, and Jane Lewin shared the editing responsibilities. Administrative and clerical support were provided by Deborah Rivers, Gina Kenion, Merlinda Novicio, and Ann Woodbury. Constance Toliver and Robert Oram were responsible for typesetting and styling.

Eddie N. Williams
President
Joint Center for Political Studies

ABOUT THE AUTHORS

L es Aspin (D-Wis.) was first elected to Congress in 1970, and has served as chair of the House Armed Services Committee since 1985. He holds a Ph.D. in economics from the Massachusetts Institute of Technology.

McGeorge Bundy is a professor of history at New York University. He served as special assistant to the president for national security from 1961 to 1966, and as president of the Ford Foundation from 1966 to 1979. His publications include *On Active Duty* (with Henry L. Stimson).

Edwin Dorn is a deputy director of research at the Joint Center for Political Studies. His publications include *Rules and Racial Equality* and articles on education, civil rights, and defense policy.

Cynthia H. Enloe is a professor of government at Clark University in Worcester, Massachusetts. Her publications, which focus on the relationship between militarism, sexism, and racism, include *Ethnic Soldiers: State Security in Divided Societies.*

Robert K. Fullinwider is a research associate at the Center for Philosophy and Public Policy University of Maryland. Among his publications is an edited volume, *Conscripts and Volunteers: Military Requirements, Social Justice and the All-Volunteer Force.*

Lawrence J. Korb is director of the Center for Public Policy Education at the Brookings Institution. From 1981 to 1985 he served as assistant secretary of defense for manpower, reserve affairs, and logistics. His publications include *The Joint Chiefs of Staff: The First Twenty-Five Years.*

Elsie Moore is a professor of psychology and education at Arizona State University. She is the co-author, with R. Darrell Bock, of *Advantage and Disadvantage: A Profile of American Youth.*

Charles C. Moskos is a professor of sociology at Northwestern University. He has conducted research on U.N. peacekeeping, civil-military relations, and national service. Among his publications are *The American Enlisted Man* and *A Call to Civic Service.*

Alvin J. Schexnider is associate vice president for academic affairs at Virginia Commonwealth University. He is a co-author of *Blacks and the Military,* published by the Brookings Institution.

A. Wade Smith is a professor of sociology at Arizona State University. He has published articles on survey research methods and the sociology of education, and has served as associate editor of the *Journal of Marriage and the Family* and of the *American Sociological Review.*

Roger Wilkins is a senior fellow at the Institute for Policy Studies in Washington, D.C., and the Clarence J. Robinson Professor of History and American Culture at George Mason University. He received a Pulitzer Prize (with Carl Bernstein, Robert Woodward, and Herblock) for the *Washington Post's* coverage of the Watergate episode. His autobiography is entitled *A Man's Life.*

1. INTRODUCTION

Edwin Dorn

P eriodically during the nation's history, racial and ethnic considerations have directly influenced decisions about defense policy and military manpower. President Woodrow Wilson's attempt at neutrality during the early years of World War I was motivated partly by his desire to avoid alienating Irish-American and German-American voters before the 1916 presidential election.[1] Shortly after entering World War II, the U.S. government sent more than 100,000 Americans of Japanese descent to internment camps and initially rejected them for military service; German-Americans and Italian-Americans were not subjected to such harsh treatment.[2]

Concerns about the role of blacks in the nation's defense surfaced with the establishment of colonial militias and caused General George Washington to issue several conflicting orders regarding blacks in the Continental Army.[3] In October 1775, the Council of War of the Continental Army voted "to reject Negroes altogether";[4] but only a few weeks later, Washington advised the Continental Congress that he "would begin recruiting free blacks and reenlisting those discarded as a result of the recent ban on accepting Negroes."[5]

General Andrew Jackson, desperate to fortify New Orleans against the British in the War of 1812, issued a ringing call for the "free colored inhabitants of Louisiana" to join "the glorious struggle."[6] Soon after that war ended, the War Department banned the recruitment of any "Negro or mulatto."[7]

At the outset of the Civil War, President Abraham Lincoln was reluctant to enlist blacks until Congress explicitly authorized him to rescind quotas and "employ as many persons of African descent as he may deem necessary and proper."[8] Approximately

Concerns about the role of blacks in the nation's defense surfaced with the establishment of colonial militias and caused General George Washington to issue several conflicting orders regarding blacks in the Continental Army.

1

180,000 blacks served in the Union Army and more than 29,000 in the Union Navy.[9]

Confusion and vacillation over the role of blacks in the military continued until well into the twentieth century. At the beginning of a conflict, blacks generally were not recruited; as war persisted, they were recruited vigorously; and once the emergency had passed, they were demobilized quickly.[10]

From the end of the Civil War to 1950, the army maintained a 10 percent quota on black enlistments. The marine corps totally banned blacks in 1798 and remained racially exclusive until early in World War II.[11] Moreover, American soldiers served in segregated units until the Korean War, and most black units were commanded by whites. Thus, blacks had few opportunities to become officers. When the country began to mobilize for World War II, for example, the regular army had only five black officers, and three of them were chaplains.[12]

Blacks themselves have had ambivalent feelings about defending a country that legally relegated them to second-class citizenship. When he was editor of the NAACP's magazine *Crisis,* W. E. B. Du Bois apparently agonized before deciding to encourage blacks to enlist during World War I. In a July 1918 editorial, he wrote, "Let us not hesitate. Let us, while the war lasts, forget our special grievances and close ranks . . . with our white fellow citizens . . . fighting for democracy."[13] He apparently reasoned that black sacrifices on the battlefield would help pave the way for greater acceptance of blacks at home. The treatment black soldiers experienced during and immediately after World War I—when several returning black servicemen were lynched while wearing the uniform of their country—may have contributed to the disillusionment that eventually caused Du Bois to leave the United States.

Blacks themselves have had ambivalent feelings about defending a country that legally relegated them to second-class citizenship.

As McGeorge Bundy reminds us in chapter 2, Du Bois was not the only black leader to become disillusioned. William Hastie resigned from the War Department when Secretary of War Henry L. Stimson refused to desegregate the armed forces during World War II. But the war against Nazism provided a propitious opportunity for other black leaders, such as

A. Philip Randolph and Walter White, to exert pressure for change. One result was President Harry Truman's Executive Order 9981, issued in 1948, which called for "equality of treatment and opportunity for all persons in the armed services without regard to race, color, religion or national origin."

Eventually, Truman's order led to the elimination of segregation and racial quotas in the armed forces. Its immediate effect, however, was to set off a two-year debate in the Truman administration over whether those things had to be done in order to provide equal opportunity. For example, Truman's secretary of the army, concerned that the elimination of quotas would cause too many blacks to enter the service, offered the president a way to restrict black representation indirectly:

> If, as a result of a fair trial of this new system, there ensues a disproportionate balance of racial strengths in the army, it is my understanding that I have your authority to return to a system which will, in effect, control enlistments by race.[14]

Military personnel experts knew that blacks tended to score lower than whites on the services' standardized enlistment examinations and that therefore the number of blacks could be controlled by "the substitution of an achievement quota for the present racial quota."[15] Under this approach, the president could have a new system that did not contain explicit racial quotas but would nevertheless have the same effect as the old one. Truman wrote "OK, HST" on the secretary's memorandum. Soon after that, the army began issuing directives that led to the elimination of segregated units and racial quotas.

It is not clear whether test scores actually have been used specifically to control black enlistments during the four decades since E.O. 9981; but the services, like other institutions in American society, have been suspected of using them in that way. In 1971, for example, the NAACP called for "a thorough reexamination" of the military's qualifications test to determine whether it was being used to restrict opportunities for black service personnel.[16]

Given this background, it is not surprising that the debate in the late 1960s and early 1970s over ending

Military personnel experts knew that blacks tended to score lower than whites on the services' standardized enlistment examinations and that therefore the number of blacks could be controlled by "the substitution of an achievement quota for the present racial quota."

3

Since the AVF came into being in 1973, the representation of blacks in the armed services has nearly doubled.

the draft and replacing it with an all-volunteer force (AVF) should have included a discussion of the AVF's probable racial composition. One key argument against the AVF was that it would become disproportionately black. That possibility was denied by its proponents. Testifying on behalf of the AVF, Defense Secretary Melvin Laird stated that "we do not foresee any significant difference between the racial composition of the all-volunteer force and the racial composition of the nation."[17]

Laird has been proven wrong. Since the AVF came into being in 1973, the representation of blacks in the armed services has nearly doubled. Blacks make up one-third or more of some army units, such as the 2d Army Division in Korea. That development has helped keep alive questions about the viability and the desirability of the AVF.[18]

This volume addresses a number of questions associated with the changing racial composition of the armed services. Although most of the chapters are based on presentations originally made at a symposium at the Wingspread Conference Center in Racine, Wisconsin, in the summer of 1982, the interval between original statement and publication has not rendered the analyses irrelevant; nor have events overtaken assessments. Some of the statistics have been updated, but the issues remain basically unchanged.

For example, when McGeorge Bundy offered his assessment of U.S.-Soviet relations, cruise missiles had not yet been installed in Germany, President Ronald Reagan had not yet announced the Strategic Defense Initiative, and Mikhail Gorbachev was not the Soviet general secretary; but his basic thesis—that the level of real tension between the United States and the Soviet Union is significantly lower than the level of rhetoric—remains intact. The recession of 1981-83 caused many more white youths to enlist (thereby reducing slightly the percentage of blacks among accessions), but black representation began rising again as the nation recovered from the recession. With black representation in the enlistment-age cohort expected to grow during the late 1980s, blacks will continue to constitute a large percentage of military personnel.

Finally, given Ronald Reagan's reelection in 1984, the defense policy outlined by former Reagan administration official Lawrence Korb—including a commitment to the AVF—remains unchanged. Korb and Representative Les Aspin (D-Wis.) agree that there is little sentiment for returning to a draft, and the 1984 elections bore out that assessment. Of the eight contenders for the Democratic presidential nomination in 1984, only one—Senator Ernest Hollings (D-N.C.)—supported conscription.

The mention of Bundy, Korb, and Aspin suggests something about the nature of this publication and about the thinking behind the Wingspread symposium. Military personnel policy is a dependent variable. Decisions about the number and quality of the people needed by the armed forces are influenced by other policy decisions about the nation's defense. What are U.S. strategic interests? How are they likely to be threatened? Is a threat imminent, and what is the capability of the potential adversaries? Only after those questions are answered can defense planners address matters such as force structure, military materiel, and manpower.

Decisions about defense policy are influenced by policy-makers' assessments not only of international circumstances but also of domestic conditions. It is one thing for military analysts to determine that an adversary is capable of, say, disrupting the supply of oil from the Middle East. It is quite another for political leaders to determine that Americans are willing to sacrifice in order to defend the country's interest in Middle Eastern oil.

This volume begins, then, with an assessment of the general levels of tension in the world and a description of the policies developed in response to them. McGeorge Bundy, who has spent more than three decades analyzing and shaping national security policy, argues that tensions between the United States and its major adversary are not abnormally high: a war with the Soviet Union is not imminent. Nor does Bundy see a fundamental difference between the defense spending policies of the Reagan administration and those of the Carter administration. The dollar figures in the Reagan defense budget—an estimated $1.6 trillion over five years—are large in

Decisions about the number and quality of the people needed by the armed forces are influenced by other policy decisions about the nation's defense. What are U.S. strategic interests? How are they likely to be threatened? Is a threat imminent, and what is the capability of the potential adversaries?

5

an absolute sense; but Bundy argues that they are not dramatically different from the defense spending plans developed during Jimmy Carter's last year in office.

Bundy also offers an observation about the debate over the representation of blacks in the armed services. For him, the concern ought not to be with the number of blacks in uniform but with the fact that large numbers of middle-class white youths are avoiding a basic obligation of citizenship.

Lawrence Korb, who served as assistant secretary of defense for manpower from 1981 to 1985, takes issue with Bundy's suggestion that "less is happening than meets the eye." He points out that some policies, such as increasing the size of the force and building new weapons systems, cannot be implemented quickly.

Korb explains the guiding principles of the administration's defense policy and offers a pointed defense of the all-volunteer force. Among other things, he argues that we should be more interested in the readiness of the force than in its racial composition. (In response to a question raised by Roger Wilkins, however, Korb concedes that some people, including some of our NATO allies, have privately expressed concern about the racial composition of U.S. forces.)

For [Bundy], the concern ought not to be with the number of blacks in uniform but with the fact that large numbers of middle-class white youths are avoiding a basic obligation of citizenship.

Representative Les Aspin offers an explicitly political assessment of the all-volunteer force. From his position as a member of the House Armed Services Committee (and the committee's chairperson in the 99th and 100th Congresses), Aspin has determined that there is little enthusiastic support on Capitol Hill for the AVF. The AVF is accepted "grudgingly" because the alternatives—a military draft either by itself or as part of a larger system of compulsory national service—are viewed as worse. One reason the AVF receives only grudging support, Aspin argues, is that "it bothers people to pay market rates for things that should be done as a matter of duty" (a concern that sociologist Charles Moskos explores in a later chapter).

Bundy, Korb, and Aspin provide rich and varied views of the policy context in which questions about blacks in the military arise. The next group of chapters examines some of those questions. Chapter 5, by Alvin Schexnider and myself, presents the statistical data. Generally speaking, black men and women make up a higher proportion of military personnel than they do of the American population. But the degree of overrepresentation (or, in some cases, of underrepresentation) varies by rank, service, and occupational specialty. In fact, in many ways the distribution of blacks within the military is similar to the distribution of blacks in the civilian labor market.

In chapter 6, Elsie Moore expands on this last point in one particular area: she examines how the quality of education that blacks receive before their enlistment influences the roles they go on to perform in the military.

Charles Moskos then tells us why we ought to be concerned about the statistics. To him, the issue is not one of race, but of class: under the AVF, the proportion of middle-class, college-educated whites (and blacks) in the enlisted ranks has declined precipitously, a trend that in his view is not in the nation's long-term interest. Moskos takes exception to a fundamental premise that he claims guides the AVF—namely, that the way to fill the ranks of the military should be by relying on economic incentives. His proposal for altering the socioeconomic and racial composition of the enlisted ranks without returning to conscription is to make some changes in the AVF's incentive structure.

In Chapter 8, Robert Fullinwider disputes two common assertions about the AVF: that the large percentage of blacks makes the AVF "unrepresentative" of American society and that enlistees are "forced" to serve by reason of economic necessity. Fullinwider argues that a heavily black force can be called unrepresentative only if we view blacks as so "alien" to the larger society that they cannot be said to reflect its basic values and interests. Few people, he suggests, really want to propose so extreme a view. As to whether blacks and poor whites have no choice but to join the military or face unemployment, Fullinwider poses a compelling rhetorical question: would we say that they had no choice if the alternative to unemployment were either a college scholarship or a job

Generally speaking, black men and women make up a higher proportion of military personnel than they do of the American population. But the degree of overrepresentation (or, in some cases, of underrepresentation) varies by rank, service, and occupational specialty.

paying $25,000 a year? Obviously, the answer is no. And if it is no, then we are not really complaining about the lack of a choice but, rather, about the nature of the choice. Those who say blacks have no choice but to serve in the military, Fullinwider concludes, are denigrating both military service and the motivations of black Americans.

> *Race will be a problem in the military until we deal with it in the larger society.*

Chapters 2-8 tell us how policy-makers and scholars view the high percentage of blacks in the military. In chapter 9, A. Wade Smith indicates what the average citizen makes of the matter. Using data from a public opinion survey, Smith finds that Americans are not nearly as concerned about the percentage of blacks in the military as some commentators have suggested they are. He also examines public opinion toward women in the military and finds that the average American would tolerate a greater role for women than is possible under current military personnel policies.

Cynthia Enloe then calls on us to recognize that a preoccupation with the racial or ethnic composition of a military force is not uniquely American. She argues that every multi-ethnic or multi-racial society, from the Soviet Union to Peru, is sensitive to such matters. Some nations have even developed elaborate "warrior race" myths to justify recruiting some groups into the military and excluding others.

Finally, Pulitzer Prize-winning journalist Roger Wilkins comments on what all this means to him and what it should mean to the larger society. He agrees that we should be concerned about who defends America. But he cautions that a focus on blacks in the military could serve as a convenient evasion—a way of discussing one manifestation of racism without confronting deeper, more pervasive issues of race. In one sense, Wilkins agrees with Lawrence Korb: race will be a problem in the military until we deal with it in the larger society.

Endnotes

1. Arthur S. Link, *Wilson Campaigns for Progressivism and Peace, 1916-1917* (Princeton: Princeton University Press, 1965). See chapter 1.

2. *Korematsu v. U.S.*, 323 US 214 (1944). See also "Personal Justice Denied," Report of the Commission on War-time Relocation and Internment of Civilians (Washington, D.C.:GPO, December 1982).

3. Benjamin Quarles, *The Negro in the American Revolution* (Chapel Hill: University of North Carolina Press, 1961), p. 8.

4. *Blacks in the Military--Essential Documents,* ed. Bernard C. Nalty and Morris J. MacGregor (Wilmington, Del.: Scholarly Resources, Inc., 1981), p. 7.

5. Nalty and MacGregor, p. 8.

6. Nalty and MacGregor, p. 16.

7. Nalty and MacGregor, p. 17.

8. Nalty and MacGregor, p. 24.

9. Benjamin Quarles, *The Negro in the Civil War* (Boston: Little, Brown and Company, 1969), p. xii.

10. John Sibley Butler and Malcolm D. Holmes, "Changing Organization Structure and the Future of Race Relations in the Military," in Robert K. Fullinwider, ed., *Conscripts and Volunteers: Military Requirements, Social Justice and the All Volunteer Force* (New York: Rowan and Littlefield, 1982).

11. Nalty and MacGregor, p. 14.

12. Ulysses Lee, *The Employment of Negro Troops* (Washington, D.C.: GPO, 1966), p. 29.

13. Quoted in Robert W. Mullen, *Blacks in America's Wars* (New York: Monad Press, 1973), p. 45.

14. Nalty and MacGregor, p. 264.

15. Nalty and MacGregor, p. 263.

16. *The Search for Military Justice: Report of an NAACP Inquiry Into the Problems of the Negro Serviceman in West Germany* (New York: NAACP Special Contribution Fund, 1971), p. 20.

17. Quoted in Martin Binkin and Mark J. Eitelberg with Alvin J. Schexnider and Marvin M. Smith, *Blacks and the Military* (Washington, D.C.: The Brookings Institution, 1982), p. 3.

18. See Binkin et al., *Blacks and the Military;* Martin Binkin, *America's Volunteer Military: Progress and Prospects* (Washington, D.C.: The Brookings Institution, 1984); Kenneth J. Coffey, *Strategic Implications of the All-Volunteer Force* (Chapel Hill: University of North Carolina Press, 1979); Alvin J. Schexnider and John Sibley Butler, "Race and the All-Volunteer System: A Reply to Janowitz and Moskos," *Armed Forces and Society* 2 (Chicago: Inter-University Seminar on Armed Forces and Society, Spring 1976); Ronald V. Dellums, "Don't Slam Door to Military," *Focus* 3 (June 1975); and Morris Janowitz, "Focus on Blacks in Military," *Focus* 3 (June 1975).

2. THE NATIONAL SECURITY CONTEXT

McGeorge Bundy

T
he topic of this study is enormously important. But it is one about which I probably know less than most of the authors who have contributed. Although I have paid close attention to the issue of race relations, particularly during the 13 years I served as president of the Ford Foundation, my exposure to the specific issue of race in the military has been somewhat limited. Indeed, one of the interesting but disturbing points I should make is that the issue of race and the military did not arise in my office very frequently while I served as national security advisor to President Kennedy.

My own interest in the issue, however, goes back to the late 1940s, when I was writing about the War Department during World War II. One of the things I had great difficulty understanding about that period was the relationship between two men in the War Department who were concerned with the race issue. One of those men was Henry Stimson, then secretary of war. The other was William Hastie, who served as Stimson's advisor on race relations. I worked for Stimson on a book about his life, and I later became a good friend of Hastie's. Those two extraordinarily good, able, determined men simply could not understand each other on the issue of race. Hastie, who later became a distinguished judge, tried to push Stimson to ensure fairer treatment for black soldiers. Stimson apparently felt the War Department was doing as much as possible in light of its one overriding obligation, which was, "dammit, [to] win the war." Hastie acted on his convictions and resigned after Stimson supported the establishment of a segregated air corps training school.

As I studied that episode, I was intrigued and saddened that those two genuinely great human

In talking about race in the United States, one can make two great mistakes. One is to think nothing has changed; the other is to think the problem has been solved.

11

beings had not been able to communicate about so important a matter. But race produced irreconcilable differences in their perspectives, and I am sure it has done so many times.

One must be impressed by the changes that have occurred since that time. I was astonished to read recently that nearly 13 percent of all officers in the U.S. Army today are members of minority groups. Even though one should assess that figure in light of other information about rank, assignment, fairness, and so forth, the figure itself is extraordinary when compared with the situation that prevailed during World War II, when Hastie and Stimson failed to understand each other.

We are in a phase—in American national security policy, in American foreign policy, and even in American military policy—when rather less is happening than meets the eye.

In talking about race in the United States, one can make two great mistakes. One is to think nothing has changed; the other is to think the problem has been solved. My guess is that when we find the right levers, including the levers that control decision-making in the military services, we will see that change can be achieved much more readily today than when William Hastie was a young man trying to resolve race issues in the old War Department. But it is enormously difficult to get people to level with one another on the subject of race. So if this study does nothing else, it can make a great contribution by encouraging people to discuss the concerns candidly and to think hard about ways of translating the issues into action.

Lowered Tension

I want now to talk about a subject with which I am more familiar—national security policy. My general proposition is this: we are in a phase—in American national security policy, in American foreign policy, and even in American military policy—when rather less is happening than meets the eye. The real changes in direction and activity are not nearly as great as the rhetoric would lead us to believe.

When historians write about the years of the Carter and Reagan administrations, I believe they will be more impressed by the continuity in national security policy than by the discontinuity. Even though substantial changes for the better probably will not be seen to have occurred, we can take comfort in the likelihood that nothing awful will have happened, either.

Why do I say this? I say it because both the Carter administration and the Reagan administration have displayed a tendency to announce changes that appear to be larger than they really are. The truth is that the overall international situation is one of relatively low tension compared with the tensions of previous decades—1945 to 1955, 1955 to 1965, and 1965 to 1975. The period between 1975 and the present has on the whole been the quietest we have experienced in the tumultuous years since World War II. In part, this is because of a certain national lassitude that developed in the aftermath of Vietnam and Watergate. But in part it is because there really has been a dramatic easing in the confrontational aspects of the Cold War.

I can make the point by putting a few recent events in perspective. First, the Soviet military buildup. We have heard a lot of talk about the Soviet buildup, and indeed there has been one. It occurred during a period when our own military expenditures were either stationary or declining, and this may have exaggerated our perception of its magnitude. In assessing the buildup, however, we need to consider Soviet perceptions. My hunch is that Soviet officials do not see this as a period during which they have achieved a significant military advantage over the United States.

Second, Soviet actions, the most dramatic of which have occurred in Afghanistan and Poland. We were taken by surprise when the Soviet Union moved troops into Afghanistan in 1979. But we should keep in mind that, at least from the Western point of view, Afghanistan has been a no-man's land ever since the British left the Khyber Pass. Although we may regret the Soviet incursion, we should not regard it as a matter that dramatically affects the balance in international influence between East and West. We also are dismayed at the Soviet Union's role in suppressing the development of free trade unions in Poland. Poland, however, has been a part of the Soviet sphere of influence since the end of World War II, and the

The truth is that the overall international situation is one of relatively low tension compared with the tensions of previous decades.

13

probability that the Soviets would reassert their influence there has always been very great.

The notion that eight-foot-tall Russians are coming figured heavily in the rhetoric of the Reagan administration before and shortly after it took power. In the administration's current public posture, however, that notion is receding very conspicuously. I think the trend suggests that the president has accommodated himself to the reality that selling grain to the Soviets is preferable to confronting them. It also reflects the reality that the American public prefers a less confrontational approach.

Third, the Iranian hostage incident. That was one of the most dramatic international events to occur during the Carter administration. It was humiliating to the nation and painful to all those who were directly involved. It may have affected the 1980 presidential election. Despite the pain and humiliation that the taking of the hostages caused, however, the incident was trivial in the larger context of international affairs. Even recognizing the human suffering that the Iranian incident entailed, I believe that an age in which such an event can figure so prominently will appear in history to have been a lucky age.

Therefore, although the current strategic debate is important—and although indeed it has to do with issues of survival—it is *not* taking place in an environment of imminent crisis. I say this with all deference to those who are trying to raise public consciousness about the potential for nuclear destruction and the destabilizing effects of new weapons systems. Ironically, the administration's position in the nuclear debate gives us cause for optimism. Each new MX missile scheme, for example, is less plausible than the last one, which gives us hope that during the next five years the whole idea of the MX may collapse under the weight of its own implausibility.

Although the current strategic debate is important—and although indeed it has to do with issues of survival—it is not taking place in an environment of imminent crisis.

This is not to make light of the issues. It is simply to suggest that many of the disagreements over defense strategy are not as great as the speakers on each side would lead us to believe. I do not think, for example, that the so-called window of vulnerability has much meaning even for the people who mention it frequently. Nor do I believe that the window of vulnerability, if such a thing exists, will affect the future of national strategic issues. The nuclear balance of terror, unsatisfactory as it is as a permanent solution, is stable. It is viewed as stable by responsible people in both Washington and Moscow. The level of tension—as distinct from the level of rhetoric—between the United States and the Soviet Union is not, as I have shown, abnormally high. At this very moment, the summer of 1982, tensions are much lower than they were on a number of occasions during the 1970s.

Nevertheless, a time of quiet is not necessarily a time for inactivity, and certainly not a time for the absence of thought. This is precisely when we need to think deeply about the question of nuclear war. I am encouraged, therefore, by the public's increasing awareness that living by thermonuclear deterrence is a very dangerous form of survival. But it will take time for this heightened public understanding to be translated into significant changes in policy: it will require, among other things, changes in the types of people who run the executive branch of government, and those changes are not likely to occur on a large scale in the near future.

I am encouraged by the public's increasing awareness that living by thermonuclear deterrence is a very dangerous form of survival. But it will take time for this heightened public understanding to be translated into significant changes in policy.

A Stable Defense Budget

I have suggested that there is greater continuity than discontinuity in our approach to international affairs. The same is true about the defense budget and about allocations within the defense budget. Changes have been proposed, and they will be hotly debated. But they will be debated within a relatively narrow range—narrow in comparison with the magnitudes of either the defense increases that occurred under the shock of the first Soviet nuclear test in 1949 or the military buildups that occurred in response to Korea, Berlin in 1961, and Vietnam. Substantial pressure exists, for example, to reduce the relatively high spending targets set by the secretary of defense early in 1981, just as substantial pressure existed to increase the relatively low targets initially set by President Carter.

15

My guess is that the outcome of the debate will be a real annual increase in the defense budget falling somewhere between 4 percent (which was the goal set by President Carter near the end of the SALT II ratification debate) and perhaps 6 or 7 percent. My point is that a 2 or 3 percentage point difference in the rate at which the annual defense budget grows does not indicate a major change in the nation's overall defense posture.

As we think about the future, therefore, it is wise to think in terms of a relatively stable military budget taking shape during a relatively calm period in international affairs. Any such prediction is, of course, subject to contradiction by events: in international affairs, the unexpected is in a sense the predictable. Clearly, the largest and most uncertain region of risk is the Middle East, as has long been the case. But I do not think that in Europe during the next few years there is going to be an explosion of military danger, nor do I think there will be so great a revolution in our relations with China that we will find ourselves at war in the Far East.

Changes in Military Manpower?

If this is true, then—coming back to the question we began with—we are not likely to see any major changes in the military manpower situation in the immediate future. The president and the secretary of defense are firmly committed to making the all-volunteer force work, and no strong political pressure is building up for a return to the draft. However, my instinctive feeling is that in the long run, that may change.

A s we think about the future, therefore, it is wise to think in terms of a relatively stable military budget taking shape during a relatively calm period in international affairs.

My view of military service is marked by the experience of my generation, the last generation in which virtually every able-bodied male was called to war. Unfair as war is—and war was what taught John Kennedy that life is unfair—I do see some broad social value in military service. Military service helps to develop a sense of shared exposure, a sense of affirmative connection among the various parts of our society.

I am troubled by the distance that developed between the American military and the universities

16

during the 1960s, and I do not think this sense of alienation has been sorted out. I would go further, to suggest that the failure lies more on the civilian side than on the military side. I think nearly any average field grade officer, for example, would be more tolerant of the editors of the *Village Voice* than vice versa. That may be an extreme example, but the general problem is widespread.

I am not impressed by the children of highly privileged white families who think that the right way to criticize the military is to stay light years away from military service and to fail to inform themselves about what it takes to make the armed forces effective. Nor am I the least bit troubled that blacks are playing a quantitatively larger role in the military today than they have played before. I can only hope that, with this study, policymakers will pay close attention to the qualitative aspects of black participation and to the rewards their military participation merits. With or without a volunteer force, people need rewards and incentives for military service—although the rewards do not necessarily have to fol-low the standards of the marketplace. Properly designed educational incentives, for example, may prove an effective way to ensure participation in the military.

It is enormously important that we work harder to establish effective connections between the military and the civilian parts of our society. One way to do that is by participation in military service. During a period of relative international tranquility, when only a small percentage of citizens actually serve in the military, the problem of developing those connections becomes even more difficult, but also more important.

I am not impressed by the children of highly privileged white families who think that the right way to criticize the military is to stay light years away from military service and to fail to inform themselves about what it takes to make the armed forces effective.

3. THE PENTAGON'S PERSPECTIVE

Lawrence J. Korb

M cGeorge Bundy has argued that the defense policy being pursued by the Reagan administration is very similar to the policy of the Carter administration. I suspect that both President Reagan and former President Carter would be surprised to hear that assessment, although historians possibly will discover that the similarities were indeed more pronounced than the differences.

I want to begin by describing the Reagan administration's broad national defense objectives and then explore some specific issues associated with our military personnel policy and, in particular, with the all-volunteer force. My focus will be on conventional forces rather than strategic or nuclear forces. Although the strategic forces obviously are important, they do not have tremendous implications for personnel, except to the extent that increasing or decreasing strategic forces has an effect on the level of conventional forces. Fewer than 10 percent of the more than 2 million people on active duty are assigned to the strategic nuclear forces; and the strategic package announced by President Reagan in 1981 will amount to no more than 4 percent of the defense budget by 1986. In contrast, costs associated with paying, training, and equipping personnel in the conventional or non-nuclear forces will amount to approximately 70 percent of the defense budget. Manpower is clearly the most expensive item in the defense budget.

National Defense Objectives

In the area of conventional defense, our policy is based on two considerations. First, we want the capability of fighting in Europe and also the capability of fighting someplace else without drawing from our European forces. To fight in Europe we must be

The reason for increasing our capability of sustaining a conventional war is simple: to reduce the need for using nuclear weapons.

19

able to deploy 10 army divisions to the central front, plus marine forces on the northern flank and naval forces on the southern flank. When we mention a second area of fighting, people generally think of the Persian Gulf region, but that is not necessarily correct. The rapid deployment force, when it becomes fully operational, will be able to go to the Persian Gulf or to other places in the world. Whether one describes this as "one-and-a-half wars" or "one-and-three-quarter wars" is a matter of semantics.

Second, we want to be able to fight a long war, although there is no fixed boundary between a long war and a short one. When the Reagan administration entered office, the United States was capable of fighting a conventional war in Europe for perhaps two weeks, or a month at the most. At the end of two weeks, we would have begun to run out of certain categories of weapons. The Reagan administration wants to develop the capability of fighting for two months by the middle of the decade and sustaining a conventional conflict for three months by the end of the decade.

Ironically, many of the people who express such great concern about the possibility of nuclear war also argue against a buildup of conventional forces. I find that position inconsistent.

The reason for increasing our capability of sustaining a conventional war is simple: to reduce the need for using nuclear weapons. It is possible, of course, that a European war would be short. Many analysts argue that the days of long wars are past because of the immense destructive power of current conventional weapons. But if the war were not short and if we did not have the capability of fighting a long conventional war, we would be confronted with an unacceptable choice: to capitulate or to escalate into nuclear war. That is not the type of choice we would like the commander-in-chief to have to make. Ironically, many of the people who express such great concern about the possibility of nuclear war also argue against a buildup of conventional forces. I find that position inconsistent.

Military Personnel Policy

Thus, our current military personnel needs are based on a desire to be able to fight in Europe and someplace else simultaneously and to be able to fight a long war. Our personnel policy is also based on a third factor—the military's limited ability to absorb people. Its ability is limited by the capacity of training facilities and by the availability of equipment. Many people who comment on military manpower policy overlook the fact that getting people is simply not enough. We also have to train and equip them.

Taking into consideration our general defense policy and the limitations on the military's ability to absorb people, we plan to expand the total force by 10 percent by 1987. Notice that I said *total* force. The term is important because some people have a tendency to look only at the numbers of people on active duty. Right now, the U.S. military has about 2 million men and women on active duty, 1 million in the selected reserves, another 500,000 in the individual ready reserve, and approximately 100,000 mobilization augmentees. The selected reserves are "weekend warriors," people who drill one weekend each month and spend a couple of weeks at summer camp each year. The people in the individual ready reserve still have a military service obligation; they can be recalled to active duty, but they do not belong to organized reserve units. Finally, the mobilization augmentees are career military retirees who can be recalled because they have not completed 30 years of service. In sum, we have from 3.5 million to 4 million people in the total force, and our plan is to increase that by about 10 percent between now and 1987.

We have not determined precisely how the increase will be distributed, and the numbers will probably change from year to year depending on budgets, equipment schedules, and priorities. Unfortunately, the public has become confused by premature reports. In the summer of 1981, for example, the *Washington Post* reported that the army was going to expand its personnel by 200,000. That projection had been contained in a draft planning paper; but by the time we analyzed the projection carefully and looked at the costs involved, we reduced the figure considerably. During the next few years, the number of active duty army personnel will expand not by 200,000 but by about 35,000. We will add approximately 300,000 to the total force. In the short run, much of that increase

Many people who comment on military manpower policy overlook the fact that getting people is simply not enough. We also have to train and equip them.

will be concentrated in the navy and the air force; the army is putting a higher priority on obtaining equipment. (The exact mix of active and reserve forces will be up to the individual services to determine.)

This administration is firmly committed to obtaining military personnel on a volunteer basis. The president and the secretary of defense have stated their support for the concept of the all-volunteer force (AVF). Further, as McGeorge Bundy has pointed out, there is no political consensus supporting an alternative to the AVF.

Criticisms of the AVF

In its first decade of existence, the all-volunteer force was subjected to a number of criticisms—that it was too black, too female, too dumb, too small, too expensive, and had too few reserves. In addition, allegations were made that we would not be able to obtain enough volunteers in the coming years because the pool of enlistment-age youths is declining and the economy will improve. Let me go through all of those criticisms and tell you what I think about them and how I believe the issues ought to be framed.

Black representation among enlisted personnel has been increasing, so that now approximately 20 percent of the active duty enlisted personnel are black. In the army, 30 percent of the enlisted men are black. If the armed forces of the United States were perfectly representative, around 13 percent of the force would be black because that is the proportion of blacks in the enlistment-age population.

Until civilian society gives blacks the types of opportunities that are available in the military, blacks will continue to enlist and reenlist in large numbers.

However, the growth in black representation is beginning to level off. In 1981, Jack Anderson printed an article urging the president to return to conscription because the military was attracting too many blacks. Apparently Anderson found some old data, used some straight-line projections, and concluded that by 1983, 48 percent of the force would be black. This is not going to happen; the latest data show a downward trend in the percentage of enlistees who are black. In 1981, the figures for black enlistees were 19 percent overall and 27 percent for the army. So far in 1982, the figures for all branches and for the army are 18 and 24 percent, respectively.

When people talk about the representation of blacks in the military, they tend to focus on only one part of the issue—enlistments. But the reenlistment rate for blacks is also dramatically higher—about 20 percentage points higher—than the reenlistment rate for whites. This difference has existed for the past two decades. During conscription, when the reenlistment rate among whites was 40 percent, for example, the rate for blacks was 60 percent. During conscription, though, that difference did not have a major effect on the overall representation of blacks in the military because the number of black personnel on active duty was far smaller.

Now, how does the Department of Defense feel about this? What are our concerns? Our primary concern is readiness. Neither our allies nor our adversaries are going to be concerned about the social composition of the U.S. armed forces. What they want to know is whether the U.S. armed forces can fight. That is the key issue.

Obviously, we are concerned about another issue as well—the relationship between the military and civilian society. We are aware that some people are bothered by the high percentage of blacks.* In my view, however, the cures for the problem—if it is a problem—are worse than the disease.

I would submit that until civilian society gives blacks the types of opportunities that are available in the military, blacks will continue to enlist and reenlist in large numbers. I am very frustrated with those politicians who insist they are concerned about the percentage of blacks in the military but take no

The reenlistment rate for blacks is also dramatically higher—about 20 percentage points higher—than the reenlistment rate for whites.

---

*Editor's note. In response to a question from Roger Wilkins during the conference, Dr. Korb said that people in some Allied countries, notably the Federal Republic of Germany, had privately communicated to him their concern over the number of blacks in the U.S. armed forces. "They are uncomfortable with having large numbers of black servicemen in their countries," Korb conceded, "and they would like us to return to the draft because they think a draft would reduce the percentage of blacks." Although this comment was initially made off the record, it provoked such extensive discussion that reporter Winston Williams included it in a story the *New York Times* published on June 6, 1982.

action to improve opportunities for blacks in other parts of society.

Some people argue that we can change the composition of the armed forces by returning to conscription. But conscription would dramatically alter racial composition only if we also prohibited people from volunteering, put a quota on the percentage of blacks who were allowed to volunteer, or, even worse, put a quota on their reenlistment.

We take about 350,000 people into the active force each year. The vast majority of these are true volunteers, people who want to enlist because of family tradition or because they want to travel or improve the circumstances of their lives. Even if we decided to use conscription, only a small percentage of the total force would need to be conscripted. Thus, returning to conscription would not greatly change the racial composition.

Further, one should keep in mind that blacks are not overrepresented in the total force. The percentage of blacks in the reserves is not as high as in the active duty forces. Indeed, blacks are underrepresented in some National Guard units. Since the reserve units have specific functions in time of war, one must take them into consideration.

When the all-volunteer force was instituted, women represented about 1.5 percent of military personnel; they now make up about 9 percent. The increase is the result of two factors. First, the services had problems recruiting enough men during the 1970s. Commanders experienced no great dawning of enlightenment that led them to become philosophically committed to increasing the opportunities for women. They simply had problems finding sufficient numbers of men who wanted to enlist. Second, the women's movement inspired women to press harder for admission to the military as part of the opening up of nontraditional career opportunities. The latter factor was the more important of the two.

I do not think there are too many women in the services, although I suspect that some senior military officers have misread the administration's signals on

> *Some people argue that we can change the composition of the armed forces by returning to conscription. But [that would work] only if we also prohibited people from volunteering, put a quota on the percentage of blacks allowed to volunteer, or, even worse, put a quota on their reenlistment.*

this point. President Reagan opposed the Equal Rights Amendment, and a number of military planners assumed that he was also concerned about women in the military. The result was a great rush among the services to alter their plans for admitting more women.

A number of studies of the effects of women in the services have found no conclusive evidence that a high percentage of women reduces readiness. In my view, women actually increase readiness, since they have more education and higher aptitudes than their male counterparts. But we hear a lot of anecdotes about women tending to be absent from duty for medical reasons more frequently than men. Those anecdotes, though, overlook the fact that men are frequently absent for more "traditional" reasons—being drunk and disorderly, for example. When I point this out, people tend to dismiss it by saying, "Well, we don't count that because boys will be boys."

The only gender-specific problem we have been able to identify is pregnancy, and even this problem tends to be distorted. An ABC News correspondent once interviewed me just after he had been out in the field listening to a lot of horror stories about women. He insisted that there were too many women. We went back and forth on the issue. I cited the evidence; he cited the anecdotes. Finally, he looked at me in exasperation and said, "Well, can you deny that women have a higher pregnancy rate than men?" Needless to say, that exchange did not make it onto the airwaves.

There is, however, one issue involving women that we must confront: the combat-exclusion policy. We have that policy because people in this society simply do not wish to send women into combat, where they will die in large numbers. Unfortunately, the combat-exclusion policy has created the worst of all possible worlds for female military personnel.

For example, a woman in the air force cannot fly a fighter or a bomber because those are classified as combat aircraft. But she can fly or serve as a crew member on a tanker. Now, in a combat situation, the prudent enemy is more likely to fire at a tanker than

In my view, women actually increase readiness, since they have more education and higher aptitudes than their male counterparts.

25

at a fighter or a bomber because if he shoots down the tanker, the other aircraft cannot reach their targets. In effect, then, the woman may be at greater risk. In addition, she is prevented from advancing through the ranks as rapidly as a man because the way to get ahead in the air force is to fly combat aircraft. Another example: a woman can serve as an air controller on an air force base in Europe, but she cannot serve as an air controller on a navy ship that may be thousands of miles from the combat zone.

If we want to raise the representation of women in the military above the current level of 9 or 10 percent, we are going to have to modify the combat-exclusion policy. However, policy-makers are reluctant to talk about it. Congress clearly will not address it; a change of that sort would not even get past the committee level. So we are at about 10 percent and holding until society makes up its mind about the combat-exclusion policy.

In chapter 6, Elsie Moore examines the *Profile of American Youth,* a study that compares the educational achievement and trainability of the general youth population with the educational achievement and trainability of the people who are enlisting in the military. Let me say a couple of things about this issue. Frequently, comparisons between military enlistees and the civilian population are distorted because they compare enlistees with a civilian population that contains large numbers of college graduates.

If we want to raise the representation of women in the military above the current level of 9 or 10 percent, we are going to have to modify the combat-exclusion policy.

Even so, the military does not come out badly. Our study shows that whereas 74 percent of the enlistment-age population are high school graduates, about 80 percent of the people we take into the military have high school diplomas. The aptitude (or trainability) scores of military enlistees are slightly higher than those of the youth population at large. Generally, the all-volunteer force is fairly representative of civilian society in all demographic characteristics except race and sex.

A number of people argue that the enlisted force should have more college graduates. I am not convinced of that. College graduates are overqualified for most of the jobs that enlisted personnel perform. When people are overqualified, they tend to become frustrated. College graduates should be directed into the officer corps, just as private industry directs its college-educated job applicants toward white-collar positions. General Motors would not take college graduates and put them on assembly lines. Incidentally, a number of enlisted personnel complete college while they are in the service. About 5 percent enter with college degrees, but about 10 percent have completed college by the time they leave the military.

When the all-volunteer force was established, the active duty force had dropped to about 2 million; it is approaching 2.1 million today. And under President Reagan, it will probably not exceed 2.3 million, even given the administration's emphasis on increasing defense capability. That is small, but you must understand the reasons. First, people are staying in the service longer, and with lower turnover we can afford to have a smaller training base. Conscripts have a reenlistment rate of about 10 percent. The reenlistment rate of first-term volunteers is better than 50 percent.

Second, I want to reemphasize an earlier point about the speed at which a military force can be expanded. We simply do not have the equipment or training base to accommodate significantly more personnel. For most of 1981 the army could have taken in an additional 10,000 or so qualified people, but toward the end of the year the army ran out of money; it had neither the funds nor the capacity to train more enlistees.

Some argue that we could return to conscription, pay lower salaries, and use the savings to buy more equipment. Let me put the matter in proper context. First, if you want people to reenlist and become careerists, you have to pay them. For better or worse, people will not play baseball, act in the movies, or stay in the military unless they are paid what they feel is a competitive wage.

Consider what happened in 1981 when the air traffic controllers went on strike. The president ordered about 1,000 military air controllers to work at civilian airports. The average pay of a civilian air

Some argue that we could return to conscription, pay lower salaries, and use the savings to buy more equipment. . . . [But] if you want people to reenlist and become careerists, you have to pay them.

27

A return to conscription would produce high personnel turnover, which would cause an increase in training costs.

controller is about $33,000, whereas an air traffic controller in the military makes about $13,000 plus benefits. About 2,500 of the military's 10,000 air controllers come up for reenlistment each year, and we anticipated that a number of them would be tempted to resign and double their salaries by working for the FAA. Therefore, I gave permission to offer bonuses for controllers who reenlisted. Bonuses can reach as high as $16,000 for people with critical skills. When the bonuses were offered, the reenlistment rate—normally about 40 percent—went up to 60 percent.

Does this mean that careerists are unpatriotic or mercenary? No, it simply means they have common sense. When we deployed the navy to the Indian Ocean in the late 1970s, reenlistments went down precipitously. We tripled sea pay, and now people do not want to leave the ships. So the first point is that we have to pay the career force.

Second, a return to conscription would produce high personnel turnover, which would cause an increase in training costs. Our training budget for the all-volunteer force is $12 billion a year. Today's soldiers are using more sophisticated equipment, so training costs are high. If people were to stay in the military for only two years, the training costs would be increased greatly.

How, then, could conscription save money? The only way to do it would be to depress first-year pay. But keep in mind that only a small percentage of the youth population would be conscripted. So those who were conscripted would be twice "blessed": we would take two years out of their lives, and we would not pay them a decent wage.

Some critics also argue that the reserve force is too small. Recently, a man riding next to me on an airplane said, "The reserves are 250,000 people short." He was talking about the individual ready reserve, not the selected reserve. It is important to distinguish between the two. The selected reserve, which includes the Army Reserve, the Air Force Reserve, the Naval Reserve, and the National Guard units, is bigger now than it was when the all-volunteer force was established. A decade ago, about 900,000 people were in the selected reserve; about 1 million people will be in it by the end of fiscal year 1982. We will expand it to the extent that we can, but at the moment we simply do not have the equipment to support a much larger selected reserve.

There is a shortage in the individual ready reserve, but that problem should be put in context. This reserve group consists of people who leave active duty before completing their military service obligation—for example, people who entered the military during the 1960s and incurred a six-year service obligation but served only two or three years of active duty. Many people were in that group, but the vast majority of them probably did not know they were still obligated, and many of those could not be located once they left the service. On a couple of occasions, the military tried to recall members of that reserve for training. They complained to their representatives in Congress—"Hey, I've done my time"—and the representatives told the military to forget it. Therefore, although 1.3 million people were in the individual ready reserve, the services did not know where most of them were or what kind of shape they were in.

Furthermore, the reason the individual ready reserve was so large during conscription was that turnover in the active duty force was high. With the all-volunteer force, people have been remaining on active duty longer, and, as a result, the individual ready reserve has been shrinking.

We are using several approaches to build up the individual ready reserve. We are trying to get the military service obligation extended to eight years.* We are trying to include in the individual ready reserve people who reenlisted once and then left the service. And finally, Congress has given us permission to bring ready reservists back for training. Since we are now dealing exclusively with volunteers, that should be easier to do.

Finally, there is the argument that we will have difficulty obtaining sufficient numbers of volunteers when the economy improves. The economy, however, does not affect recruitment as much as many

With the all-volunteer force, people have been remaining on active duty longer, and, as a result, the individual ready reserve has been shrinking.

---

*Editor's note. This was done in 1983.

people think. In 1980, the recession had already hit the teenage labor market, and unemployment among 16- to 21-year-olds was 15.8 percent. Nevertheless, 1980 was the army's worst recruiting year; fewer than 50 percent of the enlistees were high school graduates. The next year, 1981, was the army's best recruiting year, but unemployment among youths had risen only slightly, to 17.6 percent. That modest increase in youth unemployment does not explain the dramatic improvement in recruiting. Still, an improvement in the economy probably will make recruiting tougher.

The key to avoiding the problem is retention. In the late 1970s the military services, particularly the army, had problems because the retention rate went down and the demand for recruits had to be increased. When the military loses a person with, say, 10 years' experience, it has to bring in from four to six people to replace him or her because only a small percentage of enlistees will make it all the way through the process. If retention stays up, the demand for recruits will go down.

Making the AVF Work

When the military loses a person with, say, 10 years' experience, it has to bring in from four to six people to replace him or her because only a small percentage of enlistees will make it all the way through the process.

Can we make the all-volunteer force work? I believe we can, assuming certain things. First, we have to maintain a competitive pay scale. If we cannot offer a competitive wage, retention will be hurt and the demands on recruiting will increase. (Incidentally, competitiveness of pay is as much in the eye of the beholder as it is in actual market conditions.) We will also have to use management tools such as flexible bonuses to deal with situations like the one with the military air traffic controllers.

An example of a competitive wage is the $75,000 a year in total compensation we pay the captain of a nuclear submarine, which is more than we pay the secretary of defense. Why do we pay the captain so much? Because that is what it takes to get someone to spend almost 15 consecutive years on sea duty and undergo the rigorous training required for serving on a submarine at sea. If we did not offer that type of financial reward, the submarine officer might leave the military and we would have to spend a million dollars training his replacement.

The army, in particular, must be given a competitive edge in the recruiting process because getting people to volunteer for areas like the infantry is difficult. If there are no bonuses, all of the brightest people will go into the air force and the navy, where the work is comparatively cleaner and safer and more glamorous. In 1982, 25,000 people who enlist in the army's combat arms can receive up to $20,000 worth of educational benefits apiece after four years of service. We no longer call it a GI Bill, but it is a generous education package by any name.

The army, in particular, must be given a competitive edge in the recruiting process because getting people to volunteer for areas like the infantry is difficult.

Second, to make the all-volunteer force work we have to keep it ready. In the 1970s, we let readiness deteriorate by failing to buy spare parts and failing to worry about the quality of the soldiers' lives. Instead, we spent money on exotic weapons, and people left the service in disgust.

Third, we must have the support of the American people. We will not have a high-quality force on either a volunteer or a conscription basis unless military service is perceived as an honorable occupation. There has to be a certain amount of psychic income.

Fourth, we must avoid imposing unnecessary constraints on recruiting. For example, Congress has decided that as of 1982, no more than 25 percent of enlistees can be in category IV, the lowest aptitude category the services are allowed to accept. In 1983, no more than 20 percent of enlistees can be in category IV. Even with those constraints, however, the services are doing well. Whereas in 1980, 50 percent of the army's enlistees were in category IV, so far in 1982 only 18 percent are in that category—a dramatic improvement.

In my view, the congressionally mandated quality constraints are part of an attempt to undermine the all-volunteer force without confronting the issue directly; that is, if the military cannot meet its goals, the failure can be used to justify a return to conscription. I say that because it is difficult to show that the presence of a certain percentage of category IV people in a unit actually affects combat readiness.

31

Instead of imposing that type of constraint, Congress should allow the executive branch to recruit people on the basis of whatever criteria the military feels are necessary and should then hold us accountable for the readiness of the force.

Finally, we must face the difficult questions honestly and openly. That is why studies like this are so valuable. If we want conscription, we should debate it on its merits, not try to sneak it in through the back door of national service. Nor should we try to tie military service to eligibility for college student financial aid. Society has to decide what it wants to do with higher education and what it wants to do with the military, but the two should not necessarily be tied together.

> *If we want conscription, we should debate it on its merits, not try to sneak it in through the back door of national service. Nor should we try to tie military service to eligibility for college student financial aid.*

The need for honesty applies particularly to questions about the role of blacks and women. If we were to go to war, we could expect 30 percent of the casualties to be blacks and 5 percent to be women. We cannot get around that; we have to face up to it and decide what to do about the situation.

If we face the issues directly and honestly, we can meet our military personnel needs in ways consistent with this nation's history and current political conditions.

4. A VIEW FROM CAPITOL HILL

Les Aspin

I would like to focus on the all-volunteer force and how it is viewed on Capitol Hill. Right now, the heat is off the volunteer force. As even its most severe critics will acknowledge, quantity is up, quality is up, and things are going well. As the critics point out, however, the all-volunteer force is working well right now because of some rather special circumstances. Some things are lying in wait that have many people worried about its ability to operate well in the long run. Moreover, discontent with the all-volunteer force leads people to favor alternatives that are themselves flawed.

One special circumstance is that military pay was raised considerably in the early 1980s—in October 1980 and again in October 1981—and those raises had a clear effect on the quantity and quality of recruits. Second, of course, we are in a deep recession. Unemployment, as the headlines point out, has hit a post-World War II high. If those conditions could not make the all-volunteer force work, God knows what would. But it is working.

The Critics' Complaints

So the critics of the all-volunteer force are still lying low, but they are going to make themselves known eventually. On the surface, their arguments seem to rely on statistics. Underlying the statistics, however, are many assumptions about youth and the role of military service.

The rational arguments against the all-volunteer force are that it is too dumb, too small, too black, and too expensive. In addition, the claim is made that the pool of people who will have to be enticed into an all-volunteer force—the cohort of 18-year-olds—is

The rational arguments against the all-volunteer force are that it is too dumb, too small, too black, and too expensive.

getting smaller. The size of this pool peaked in 1979 and has been going down ever since. It will rise again in the mid-1990s. The real problem-years will be the early 1990s, when a very high percentage of the people who will then be 18 years old will have to be persuaded to join the armed services. For this period the critics predict doom, although many people have argued that the all-volunteer force can be made to work and that the problem of the shrinking cohort can be overcome.

But the all-volunteer force bothers some people on a deeper, visceral plane. They are bothered a great deal at paying young men and women market wages to do something that they think ought to be done as a matter of service and not for monetary reward. They feel military service should be something more than just another job, and, to them, the all-volunteer force has turned the military into just another employer that a high school senior looks at when reviewing the available opportunities: should I work at a grocery checkout counter, drive a delivery truck, or join the military? Because the pay is good, many young men and women join the armed services. This bothers some people very much, and enlistment bonuses bother them even more. The bonuses, which many people see as equivalent to buying meat on the hoof, really stick in the craw of a great number of congressmen.

The all-volunteer force bothers some people on a deeper, visceral plane. They are bothered a great deal at paying young men and women market wages to do something that they think ought to be done as a matter of service and not for monetary reward.

Also on a visceral plane, many congressmen associate the all-volunteer force with an era of permissiveness that is no longer in fashion. They associate it with the late 1960s, an era of long hair and rock music. These congressmen feel we had to establish the all-volunteer force because in those days young people had lost their feelings of patriotism. The country was in revolt, and the military responded with the all-volunteer force. But now that the revolt is over, many people would like to change the system.

To attract volunteers, life in the military had to be made more pleasant. And somehow the idea of making the military pleasant is at odds—in the minds of many—with the need for an effective fighting force. If life in the military is pleasant enough to draw recruits, those critics think, then the United States is not going to have a tough military. To have

34

a tough military, you have to set permissiveness aside and put your recruits through demanding drills, hazing, and other challenges that force them into a cohesive unit. But doing that, the critics believe, will discourage recruits. To the critics, there is a basic philosophical contradiction between the real purpose of a military and the methods required to get recruits under a truly volunteer system.

Those are the factors that have been most troublesome to people who are unhappy with the all-volunteer force. I would say that such people are very numerous in Congress and that the all-volunteer force has very little outright support there. It has some grudging support from people who have looked at the alternatives and decided that the alternatives are not any better and may even be worse—but only a few people have looked carefully at these alternatives. Most people simply react against the all-volunteer force and for the draft or national service, the two most popular alternatives. And indeed, if you ask my constituents—if you were to go to a town meeting in Racine and raise the question—there, too, the all-volunteer force does not do very well on a show of hands. The draft, however, does quite well, as does national service.

I am especially struck by the number of liberals who are unhappy with the all-volunteer force and are talking about a return to the draft. This is now part of the credo of what people call neo-liberalism—tough-minded liberalism. Politically, the most "dynamite" position a presidential candidate could take today would be to come out for a nuclear freeze and a return to the draft. Such a position would put a candidate to the "right" on the issue of conventional forces and to the "left" on nuclear arms. That is where the votes are, whether or not it makes any sense substantively.

To the critics, there is a basic philosophical contradiction between the real purpose of a military and the methods required to get recruits under a truly volunteer system.

Problems With the Draft

The problem with the draft is that many of its proponents believe it will do things that it will not do. Many people think a return to the draft is going to save money. It could, but only if we were really willing—if I may put it bluntly—to screw the draft-

35

ees. It is important to remember that most of the increase in military pay came not when we instituted the all-volunteer force, but before that, in 1967, when the Rivers Amendment was passed. Mendel Rivers (D-S.C.), then-chairman of the House Armed Services Committee, argued that military pay should be comparable to civilian pay. His was an equity argument, not an argument for a volunteer force.

Those 1967 increases did not apply to the pay of first-term recruits. When the volunteer force came along in the early 1970s we doubled the pay of the first-term recruits and began to use more recruiters and advertising, but those increases in costs were relatively small. The bulk of the pay increase, therefore, has not been for recruits. The only way we could save money by going back to the draft would be if we forced people to do something against their will *and* paid them less than they could make on the outside. We would therefore be imposing a double penalty on the few individuals who were being drafted. Without that double penalty, we would not be able to save much money.

Second, a return to the draft would not, frankly, be likely to alter the composition of the forces very much—that is, not if we continued to pay people on the equity principle. The number of volunteers would remain very high, even without extensive recruiting or advertising, and we would probably end up drafting a very small percentage of the force—just the gap between the people we would normally get through the volunteer system and the military's actual personnel needs.* That small percentage of draftees would not change the composition of the force very much, whether we are talking about the ratios of blacks to whites, of high school graduates to nongraduates, or of people in category IV to people in categories I, II, and III.

We could, of course, draft to balance, but that would be a very difficult concept for Congress to wrestle with. Suppose 30 percent of the volunteers were black. Would we then say that we were going to

The only way we could save money by going back to the draft would be if we forced people to do something against their will **and** *paid them less than they could make on the outside.*

*Editor's note. In some years the recruiting shortfalls are very small—only a few thousand people.

draft only whites to make the percentage of blacks in the forces 13 percent? I do not think Congress would want to do that. A draft, therefore, is not going to alter the balance. To alter the balance, we would have to cut pay enough to discourage volunteers. Then we could draft in large numbers.

But again, we are faced with the question of equity. Could we really be so unfair as to draft people and then pay them peanuts? Drafting them, taking them for two years or 18 months, and then paying a low wage at the same time gets to the third problem: it is one thing to draft people when you are taking almost everyone, but it is another thing when you are drafting only a very small percentage of the eligible individuals. In the 1950s, the draft worked reasonably well because virtually all young males shared the experience of serving in the military. The people who turned 18 during the 1950s were born during the Depression and made up a relatively small cohort. The needs of the military were such that we were enlisting the bulk of eligible males. In that situation, a draft made some sense.

Today, however, we would be drafting only 5 to 10 percent of the people we needed, assuming we did not halve the pay or double the size of the force. That would change the whole nature of the debate. Even if we had a lottery draft without any exemptions, the draft would not be a universal experience and therefore would be unfair, despite its superficial impartiality and appearance of affecting a cross section of America. Under such circumstances, would we really want a draft?

Even if we had a lottery draft without any exemptions, the draft would not be a universal experience and therefore would be unfair, despite its superficial impartiality and appearance of affecting a cross section of America.

Problems With National Service

After the draft, the next position—and the one you hear argued most frequently in Congress and among constituents—is for national service. The argument goes, if you're going to draft only 1 in 10, let's go further and not just draft for the armed forces; let's put everybody to work. It is interesting that this appeals especially to people who somehow think Ronald Reagan's idea of getting the government off our backs and out of the economy is the answer to all our woes—the people who sincerely believe that the problem with the American economy is that government is messing it up, that we have too many taxes, too many programs, too much regulation, too much red tape, and too much government interference. These same people are advocating an incredible system of national service. To them I say, wait a minute. Stop and think. Do you really want to put everybody through the equivalent of two more years of high school with the federal government running the show?

First, what are we going to do with them all? Theoretically, there are lots of things that need to be done. But labor unions are going to say, "We've got all kinds of people unemployed here. You're drafting the kids of our members, putting them to work, and taking the jobs away from our members."

Second, there is the issue of having the federal government in charge of all of these kids. I would not want to be the congressman getting letters from mothers with complaints about drugs, about sex, about how their children are being beaten up by members of another racial or ethnic group, about how they are wasting time doing make-work. We would have millions of teenagers sitting around doing nothing and getting into all kinds of trouble. The obvious answer is to have enough supervisors, but that presents problems that I will get to in a moment. What would we do about exemptions? What would we do about those who are not really very bright—the people in category V that we do not take into the military? And what would we do about criminals or borderline criminals?

Stop and think. Do you really want to put everybody through the equivalent of two more years of high school with the federal government running the show?

The third problem is the cost, which would depend on the type of national service system we had. On the low side, we would pay inductees two-thirds of the minimum wage and have one supervisor for every 100 young people—and that is asking for trouble. We would take inductees for only six months. We might have a 60 percent qualification rate, which would mean leaving out a vast number of people. We would keep them in their home counties to avoid transportation costs and would spend only $100 per inductee for training. That stripped-down national service program would cost about $5 billion a year.

The maximum program looks like this: we would pay them the minimum wage and have a larger number of supervisors. We would draft for two years. We would have a qualification rate of 95 percent. We would allow several hundred dollars in transportation costs to move them to and from training centers, where we would spend $3,000 per inductee on training. That full-fledged system would cost around $80 billion a year.

The actual program would be somewhere in between. But is the American public, especially now when we are cutting back government expenditures, willing to come up with between $5 billion and $80 billion for this? It seems unlikely. And yet, the words roll off the tongue very easily: national service is good for what ails you.

What we are dealing with is a psychological problem [regarding the AVF]. . . . Critics jump quickly to some alternative without thinking through either the costs and problems associated with it or the likelihood of its producing the kind of force they want.

What we are dealing with is a psychological problem, which is that somehow the volunteer force just doesn't go down well. It flies squarely in the face of many people's ideas about the two issues I mentioned at the beginning: why people should be in a fighting force and what a fighting force is. People should serve because of patriotism, not money, and a fighting force should be tough. The critics jump quickly to some alternative without thinking through either the costs and problems associated with it or the likelihood of its producing the kind of force they want.

5. STATISTICAL TRENDS

Alvin J. Schexnider and Edwin Dorn

Our task is to present data on the representation and distribution of blacks in the armed services, looking first at blacks as a whole, then at black women, and finally at blacks by military unit and specialty. We attempt to present the data in a straightforward way, leaving to the authors of other chapters the responsibility of addressing the crucial "so what" questions. However, the reader is likely to draw some inferences more or less automatically, so we are obliged to offer some cautions.

First, terms such as "underrepresentation" and "overrepresentation" assume a standard of comparison. Different standards should be kept in mind for different sets of data. For example, blacks constitute 11.8 percent of the total population of the United States; but of the population aged 18 to 21, which is the age range of most first-term enlistees, blacks constitute 13.0 percent.[1] Of the population that has completed four years or more of college, blacks constitute about 7 percent—and this figure should be kept in mind when assessing the degree to which blacks are underrepresented in the officer corps, because a college education is a virtual prerequisite for commissioning.[2]

Second, our data are on the active duty forces, not the reserve components. As of September 1986, 2,156,593 men and women were on active duty; 410,901 (or 19 percent) of them were black.[3] Of the men and women in the reserve and National Guard units, approximately 271,000 (or 17 percent) were black.[4] Defense plans call for the reserve components to be activated in certain cases of military emergency or civil disturbance. Since the reserve and National Guard units are not used in precisely the same ways that active duty forces are used, some of the benefits and burdens of active service do not apply to the reserve components.

As of September 1986, 2,156,593 men and women were on active duty; 410,901 (or 19 percent) of them were black. Of the men and women in the reserve and National Guard units, approximately 271,000 (or 17 percent) were black.

41

Third, the statistics cover the period 1972 to 1986 and thus reflect changes that have occurred since 1982, when the Wingspread symposium took place. The slack labor market associated with the 1981-83 recession made the military more attractive to white youths and therefore caused a slight reduction in black representation. We expect this effect to be temporary. In the absence of major changes in military manpower policy or of continuing problems in the economy, the representation of blacks in the military is likely to remain high for the foreseeable future. Indeed, it may increase because the cohort that will reach enlistment age in the next few years contains a higher percentage of blacks (and Hispanics) than does the current youth cohort.

Trends in Representation

Figures 5-1 through 5-3 trace changes in the representation of blacks in the active forces from 1972 (the last year of conscription) through the end of fiscal year 1986. Overall, black representation nearly doubled, going from 11.1 percent to 19.1 percent, with a high of 19.8 in 1981.[5] As figure 5.1 shows, the trends vary from service to service; the army had the highest percentage of blacks in the early 1970s, and the army's trend line increased sharply throughout the 1970s. By contrast, black representation in the navy has been relatively low; at no time has the percentage of blacks in that service exceeded the percentage of blacks in the service-age population.

A comparison of figures 5-2 and 5-3 reveals that black "overrepresentation" is confined to the enlisted ranks, suggesting that black youths leaving or graduating from high school tend to find military service more attractive than white youths. According to one estimate, 42 percent of black youths who are eligible for military service actually enlist, compared with 14 percent of white youths.[6] This probably is related to the fact that the unemployment rate of black youths has been around 40 percent for much of the past decade, more than twice the rate for white youths.

Figure 5-2 shows that black representation among all enlisted personnel increased steadily for most of the 1970s, then leveled off toward the end of the decade. The figure also reveals different trends for

According to one estimate, 42 percent of black youths who are eligible for military service actually enlist, compared with 14 percent of white youths.

Figure 5-1

Blacks as a Percentage of All Active Duty Personnel, by Service and DOD-wide, 1972-1986

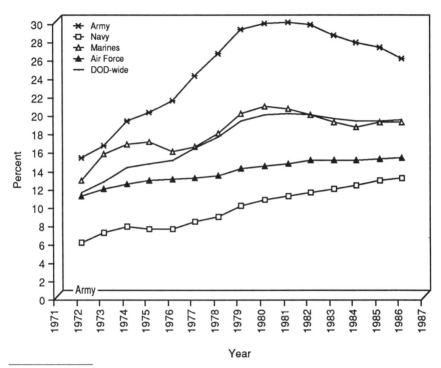

Source: Defense Manpower Data Center, Washington, D.C.

different ranks. At the entering rank (E-1), the dips in the line for blacks correspond roughly with the brief recession of the mid-1970s and with the increase in youth unemployment that preceded the 1981-83 recession. This suggests that economic downturns cause the military to become more attractive to white youths. (Whites tend to score higher on the military's standardized entry examination than blacks, so an increase in white interest tends to reduce black representation.) At the most junior non-commissioned officer level (E-4, called a corporal in the army), the modest downturn in black representation may be the result of changes in reenlistment standards. During

Figure 5-2

Blacks as a Percentage of Active Duty Enlisted Personnel, by Selected Ranks and All Ranks, 1972-1986

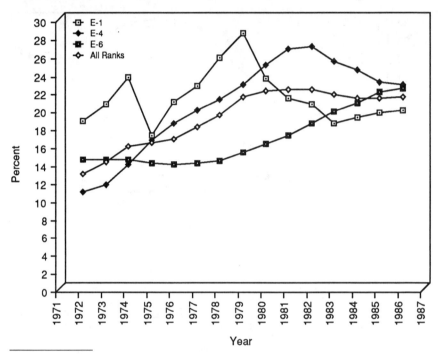

Source: Defense Manpower Data Center, Washington, D.C.

the mid-1970s, an error in grading the Armed Forces Qualification Test caused the services to admit a number of people who normally would have been rejected. It is possible that blacks were disproportionately affected when the services began to stiffen reenlistment requirements in order to correct the original enlistment error. At the more senior NCO levels (see the E-6 line in figure 5-2; generally, military personnel reach the E-6 level after four or five years of service and after their first enlistment), black representation continues to grow.

High black representation in the enlisted ranks as a whole reflects the combined effects of high black

Figure 5-3

Blacks as a Percentage of Active Duty Officer Personnel, by Selected Ranks and All Ranks, 1972-1986

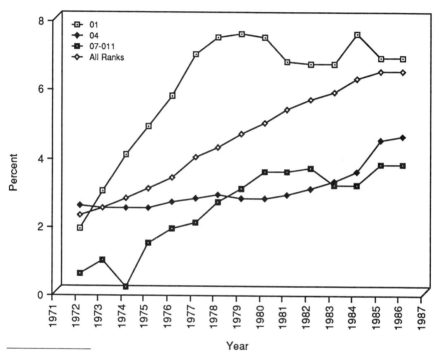

Source: Defense Manpower Data Center, Washington, D.C.

enlistment and reenlistment rates. In 1984 in the army, for example, 56.4 percent of black personnel reenlisted, compared with only 35.8 percent of white personnel.[7]

Figure 5-3 shows that in 1986, blacks made up 6.4 percent of active duty commissioned officers, a dramatic increase from the 2.2 percent of 1972.[8] If the size of the "recruitment pool" is taken into consideration—blacks are about 7 percent of the college-educated population—then blacks are not greatly underrepresented in the officer corps. As with enlisted personnel, black officers are most prominent in the army and least prominent in the navy.

Because it takes time to "make rank" in the military, it is not surprising that blacks are more heavily represented in the lower officer grades than higher up the rank structure. It takes about 10 years for an officer to move from O-1* (army second lieutenant or navy ensign) to O-4 (army major or navy lieutenant commander), and more than 20 years to move from O-1 to O-6 (army second lieutenant to colonel, or navy ensign to captain). Thus, the officers who had attained the rank of army colonel by 1986 came from the pool of officers who were commissioned in the 1960s, and that cohort contained very few blacks. The relatively large percentage of blacks who received commissions between the late 1970s and the early 1980s may help increase black representation in the senior officer grades in the 1990s. There is a countervailing trend, however: in recent years, the attrition rates of black junior officers have been higher than those of their white counterparts.[9]

Black Women in the Military

The role of women in the armed services began to change shortly after the all-volunteer force was established. In the mid-1970s, the services abolished all-female units such as the Women's Army Corps and began to integrate women into traditionally all-male units and career fields. Today, fewer than 100 of the services' more than 300 career specialties are closed to women, and those fields contain only about 10 percent of all enlisted personnel.[10] Overall, the representation of women in the active forces grew from less than 2 percent in 1972 to 10 percent in 1986.

As Lawrence Korb points out in an earlier chapter, the combat-exclusion policy—or, more specifically, the ways in which the services interpret the policy—is the major impediment to increased female representation. But other factors also come into play. For one thing, the services have had little difficulty finding male recruits in recent years, so internal pressure for change has grown less intense. For another thing, after a brief exposure to nontradi-

The relatively large percentage of blacks who received commissions between the late 1970s and the early 1980s may help increase black representation in the senior officer grades in the 1990s.

* "O" is the designation for Commissioned Officers, and "E" is the designation for enlisted personnel.

46

Figure 5-4

Black Women as a Percentage of All Active Duty Female Personnel, 1972-1986

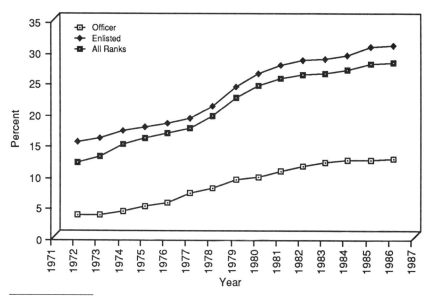

Source: Defense Manpower Data Center, Washington, D.C.

tional fields during the 1970s, many military women may themselves have chosen to build their careers around more traditional jobs—not because the women are unable or reluctant to compete with men, but because some of the jobs that men traditionally perform are unpleasant and unchallenging. Whatever the reasons, women continue to be concentrated in fields such as administration, medical services, and certain technical specialties.

Some evidence indicates that the services have been more conservative about the use of women than public opinion would justify. A survey conducted by the National Opinion Research Center in 1982 indicates, for example, that 62.4 percent of the public believes women should be permitted to serve as jet fighter pilots, and 57.4 percent believes women should be permitted to serve as crew members on

47

Table 5-1

Distribution of Blacks in the Active Duty Forces, by Service and Sex, 1986

	Both Sexes			Male			Female		
	Total	No. Black	% Black	Total	No. Black	% Black	Total	No. Black	% Black
Army									
Enlisted	667,402	197,647	29.6	597,652	167,449	28.0	69,750	30,198	43.3
Officer	94,845	9,827	10.4	83,899	7,868	9.4	10,946	1,959	17.9
Navy									
Enlisted	504,369	71,490	14.2	458,767	61,542	13.4	45,602	9,948	21.8
Officer	68,922	2,248	3.1	61,704	1,770	2.9	7,218	478	6.2
Marine Corps									
Enlisted	178,673	36,686	20.5	169,427	34,243	20.2	9,246	2,439	26.4
Officer	18,734	832	4.4	18,140	792	4.4	595	40	6.7
Air Force									
Enlisted	494,666	84,941	17.0	433,972	71,027	16.4	60,694	13,914	22.4
Officer	109,051	6,762	6.3	96,674	5,410	5.6	12,377	1,352	10.3
DOD Total									
Enlisted	1,845,110	390,764	21.2	1,660,118	334,265	20.1	185,292	56,499	30.5
Officer	291,552	18,669	6.4	290,421	14,839	5.7	31,131	3,830	12.3

Note: Table omits warrant officers; 1,468 or 7.4 percent of the 19,931 warrant officers are black.

Source: "Distribution of Active Duty Forces By Service, Rank, Sex, and Ethnic Group," September 1984, Defense Manpower Data Center, September 1986.

combat ships. In contrast, very few survey respondents believe women should be placed in units where they might become involved in hand-to-hand combat.[11]

Black women have been an important part of the changes that have occurred during the past decade. The representation of black women has grown from 11.7 percent of all active duty service women in 1972 to 27.9 percent in 1986 (figure 5-4). Change has been particularly dramatic in the army, where black women are now 43 percent of the enlisted women and 17.9 percent of the female officers.[12] As table 5-1 indicates, black women are more heavily represented in the services than black men are; this is true of both the officer and the enlisted ranks. Indeed, when we examine changes in black representation in the officer corps, we should keep in mind that a significant proportion of the improvement is traceable to increased numbers of black female officers.

Black women, like black men, are more likely than their white counterparts to enlist in the military and to reenlist. Further, black women are more likely than white women to complete their first tour of duty. In short, black women have been one of the success stories of the all-volunteer force. But as is the case with black men, the success of black women in the military may be traceable in part to a lack of viable alternatives in civilian society.

Distribution of Blacks Across Military Units and Specialties

Two important questions come to the fore in any examination of blacks in the military: are blacks in the kinds of units and jobs that would suffer heavy casualties in time of war, and are blacks obtaining the skills and experiences that will enhance their post-service employment opportunities?

As figure 5-1 revealed, blacks are more heavily represented in the army and the marine corps than in the air force and navy. The army and the marine corps tend to suffer the highest casualty rates during major conventional conflicts. If hostilities broke out in Europe or Korea, blacks might make up one-third or more of the initial casualties.[13]

But whether blacks actually would bear such a heavy burden depends upon the specifics of the conflict—where it occurs, how long it lasts, how large it becomes, and which units are engaged. In 1984, for example, blacks made up 28 percent of all army personnel. That year, of the army's 16 combat divisions, black representation was above 28 percent in 10 divisions and under it in 6. Black representation was highest (38 percent) in the 24th Infantry Division, which is stationed at Fort Stewart, Georgia, and would be used to reinforce NATO in the event of hostilities in Europe. In contrast, blacks were noticeably underrepresented in the 82d Airborne Divi-

If hostilities broke out in Europe or Korea, blacks might make up one-third or more of the initial casualties.

49

Table 5-2

Distribution of All Active Duty Enlisted Personnel, by Occupational Category and Race, 1984

Occupation	Total	Number of Blacks	Percentage Blacks
0 Infantry, guncrews, and seamanship specialists	258,897	60,708	23.4
1 Electronic equipment repairers	173,209	17,721	10.2
2 Communications and intelligence specialists	178,828	40,143	22.4
3 Medical and dental specialists	86,672	20,850	24.1
4 Other technical and allied specialists	43,513	8,004	18.4
5 Functional support and administration	285,676	91,333	32.0
6 Electrical/mechanical equipment repairers	356,913	56,102	15.7
7 Craftsmen	75,088	11,445	15.2
8 Service and supply handlers	171,236	45,533	26.6
9 Non-occupational	178,086	30,747	17.3

Source: Defense Manpower Data Center, September 1984.

sion, which is the kind of unit that might be deployed to fight limited conflicts in areas such as the Persian Gulf or Central America.[14]

In assessing the potential burdens of military service, one must keep in mind a prediction made in an earlier chapter by McGeorge Bundy: a major war in Europe or the Far East is not likely to occur. A more likely scenario, according to William J. Taylor, Jr., director of the Georgetown University Center for Strategic and International Studies, is U.S. involvement in "low-intensity conflicts in the third world."[15] These are the kinds of situations that would call, on the one hand, for the rapid deployment of highly mobile units to contain a conflict or protect specific targets such as airfields and oil refineries or, on the other hand, for the insertion of small Special Forces-type units. Such limited missions, however, always have the potential for escalating.

Answers to the question about skills development and post-career possibilities can be gleaned from table 5-2, which tells us how black enlisted personnel are distributed across the services' military occupational specialties. In 1984, blacks were heavily concentrated in routine support, administrative, service, and supply jobs (categories 5 and 8). When a young enlisted man or woman with the skills necessary for those jobs leaves the service, he or she is best qualified to serve as a secretary, clerk, truck driver, or warehouse worker. In comparison with their overall representation in the enlisted ranks, blacks are not prominent in highly technical or craft jobs.

In comparison with their overall representation in the enlisted ranks, blacks are not prominent in highly technical or craft jobs.

This does not necessarily mean that blacks gain little from serving in the military. The increasing numbers of black NCOs and senior officers suggest that large numbers of blacks are finding meaningful career opportunities in the armed services. And the fact that blacks are more heavily represented in low-skilled military specialties should be considered in light of the possibility that thousands of other young black men and women are using the military to acquire technical skills that will serve them well when they return to the civilian economy. Moreover, military service may instill a number of traits that are crucial to success in the civilian economy, such as discipline, ability to work well with others, and leadership. We hasten to point out, however, that the impact of military service on post-service employment has not been examined carefully during the period of the all-volunteer force.

Concluding Observations

Several factors combine to influence the representation of blacks in the all-volunteer force:

- the size and racial-ethnic mix of the enlistment-age population;

- the services' needs for a force of a certain size and quality;

- the condition of the civilian labor market; and

- policies affecting the role of women.

Blacks and other minorities will constitute a larger proportion of that shrinking cohort, so their representation in the armed forces is likely to increase during the 1990s.

The size of the enlistment-age population is declining, from 2.1 million 18-year-old males in 1980 to about 1.6 million in the early 1990s.[16] Blacks and other minorities will constitute a larger proportion of that shrinking cohort, so their representation in the armed forces is likely to increase during the 1990s.

Some analysts are predicting that the next decade will be a difficult one for the all-volunteer force[17] because the Defense Department is trying to maintain a force of more than 2 million active duty personnel in the face of a shrinking pool of potential male enlistees, and it is trying to upgrade the quality of personnel because military technology and tactics are growing more sophisticated.

Clearly, the lack of opportunities in the civilian economy is one reason young black men and women are joining the military in large numbers. But if the civilian economy remains healthy and blacks are "allowed in," the enlistment incentives that Lawrence Korb mentions will be put to the test. At some point, the services may find themselves in the situation that existed in the mid-1970s: needing to increase opportunities for women in order to compensate for a shortage of qualified men.[18]

Finally, there is the issue of quality. Although it may be true that in past decades the military served as an employer of last resort, currently a different picture is emerging. According to one estimate, fewer than half of the nation's young black men are qualified to join today's armed forces.[19] Moreover, many who do qualify for military duty are also capable of pursuing a college degree. It appears that for largely economic reasons—specifically, the limited availability of financial aid—black youths are choosing the armed forces over college.[20] In the following chapter, Elsie Moore explores the issue of qualifications in more detail and helps us understand why blacks are more prominent in some services and military specialties than in others.

Endnotes

1. U.S. Bureau of the Census, "General Population Characteristics," PC 80-1-B1, *U.S. Summary 1980 Census of Population* (Washington, D.C.: GPO, 1980), p. 31.

2. Derived from data in "Years of School Completed by Persons Age 18 and Over, by Age, Sex, and Race/Ethnicity, United States, 1985," *Digest of Education Statistics, 1987* (Washington, D.C.:GPO, May 1987), Table 9, pp. 14-15.

3. U.S. Department of Defense, Defense Manpower Data Center, September 1986.

4. U.S. Department of Defense, Reserve Component Common Personnel Data System (RCCPD) (September 1986).

5. Defense Manpower Data Center.

6. Mark J. Eitelberg and Brian K. Waters, "Relatively Bright and Ready to Fight: A Qualitative Comparison of Military Recruits and American Youth." Prepared for the Office of the Assistant Secretary of Defense (Manpower, Reserve Affairs and Logistics) by Human Resources Research Organization, April 1982, p. 21.

7. U.S. Department of Defense, DCSPER 597 Report, from Enlisted Soldiers Master File (Washington, D.C.: Office of Military Personnel Management, Enlisted Programs Branch, 1984).

8. Defense Manpower Data Center.

9. Edwin Dorn, "Officer Attrition," *Focus* 12 (January 1984): 1a-2a.

10. Defense Manpower Data Center.

11. James A. Davis, Jennifer Lauby, and Paul B. Sheatsley, "Americans View the Military," Report No. 131 (Chicago: National Opinion Research Center, University of Chicago, April 1983). See also A. Wade Smith, "Public Attitudes Toward the Military," *Focus* 11 (March 1983): 5.

12. Defense Manpower Data Center.

53

13. Martin Binkin and Mark J. Eitelberg with Alvin J. Schexnider and Marvin M. Smith, *Blacks and the Military* (Washington, D.C.: The Brookings Institution, 1982), p. 68.

14. Revision of DA Pamphlet 600-26, "Department of Army Affirmative Action Plan," Memorandum dated December 17, 1984. Hispanics constituted 3.8 percent of army personnel. Among combat divisions, they were concentrated most heavily in the 82d Airborne. Other minority groups, mostly Asian-Americans, make up another 4 percent of the army. Among combat divisions in 1984, they were concentrated most heavily in the 2d Infantry Division in Korea, the 25th Infantry in Hawaii, and the 7th Infantry at Fort Ord, California.

15. Introductory comments at a conference on "The Strategic Dimensions of Military Manpower," sponsored by the Center for Strategic and International Studies, May 21-22, 1985.

16. Richard V. L. Cooper, "Military Manpower Procurement Policy in the 1980s," in General Brent Scowcroft, ed., *Military Service in the United States* (Englewood Cliffs, N.J.: Prentice-Hall, 1982).

17. See, for example, Martin Binkin, *America's Volunteer Military: Progress and Prospect* (Washington, D.C.: The Brookings Institution, 1984).

18. James R. Daugherty, "Minorities and Military Recruitment," *Focus* 13 (January 1985): 3-4.

19. Binkin et al., *Blacks and the Military*, p. 98.

20. Alvin J. Schexnider, "Black Youth at the Crossroad: The Armed Forces and Higher Education," *Black Issues in Higher Education* 3:21 (February 15, 1987).

6. STANDARDIZED TESTS AND BLACK YOUTHS

Elsie Moore

In a preceding chapter, Lawrence Korb refers to a frequently heard complaint against the all-volunteer force (AVF): its enlisted ranks are "too dumb, too black, too poor, . . ." and so on. Dr. Korb rejects that complaint, and he has good grounds for doing so. A major study conducted for the Pentagon and completed early in 1982 establishes that the young men and women who are joining the military today are at least as well qualified, on average, as people in the same age group who remain in the civilian labor market. The AVF does have relatively fewer white, middle-class, college-educated enlistees than did the draft-era armed services. But little evidence has emerged to support contentions that the military has become the employer of last resort for those who could not "cut it" in the civilian labor market. This should be reassuring to the general public and to those who make defense policy.

However, when one looks more carefully at the Pentagon's study, *Profile of American Youth,* one finds that a critical social problem persists: in a country where performance on standardized tests has considerable impact on the career opportunities of young people, large, clearly identified segments of the youth population are not developing the pre-labor-market skills that will enable them to pass standardized aptitude tests at a level required for efficient assimilation into a highly technical economy.

The data clearly indicate that when scores on standardized aptitude tests are used for job selection and classification among persons of the same age, educational level, and sex, a greater percentage of white than Hispanic applicants will be selected, and the percentage of Hispanics selected will exceed that of blacks.

Little evidence has emerged to support contentions that the military has become the employer of last resort for those who could not "cut it" in the civilian labor market.

55

Some of those findings are immediately relevant to the subject we are addressing in this volume. Among other things, they may help to explain a trend mentioned by Dorn and Schexnider in chapter 5: black enlisted personnel tend to be overrepresented in the "soft," low-skilled military occupational specialties and underrepresented in the technical specialties. But beyond the implications for the military, the findings of the study also carry important implications for the larger society, since educational achievement and scores on standardized apti-tude tests are closely associated with social status and economic mobility.

My central message is that large numbers of blacks are not obtaining the quality of education needed to prepare them to do well on standardized tests and therefore to compete successfully for jobs in an increasingly demanding labor market. The point is not a new one, but the data presented below, from the Pentagon's *Profile,* allow us to examine the disparities more precisely than they have been examined previously.

Testing and Career Opportunities in America

L arge numbers of blacks are not obtaining the quality of education needed to prepare them to do well on standardized tests and therefore to compete successfully for jobs in an increasingly demanding labor market.

Standardized tests play a substantial role in both the private- and the public-sector career opportunities open to young Americans. In the private sector, an estimated 60 percent of employers with more than 25,000 employees and, at the other end of the scale, about 39 percent of employees with fewer than 100 employees use employment tests in the selection process.[1] Among governments, about three-fourths of federal, state, and local government employee merit systems use tests of some sort to select and classify personnel. And in the United States the most widely administered employment test of all is the Armed Services Vocational Aptitude Battery (ASVAB). Each year, several hundred thousand young men and women applying for military service take that battery of tests. It determines their eligibility for enlistment and their assignments to various training schools.

It is a popular misconception that "aptitude" tests such as the ones included in the ASVAB measure innate capacity and that "achievement" tests measure the effects of learning. In fact, the primary difference between the two types of test is the way they are used. Aptitude tests are used to predict *subsequent* performance (such as training school grades) and are assumed to reflect learning from the totality of the person's life experiences before testing (including learning from school). Achievement tests are usually given to determine the individual's level of mastery *after* a specific learning experience, such as a course in French.[2] Obviously, however, aptitude and achievement are related. Once we know a person's level of mastery (achievement) in a given subject, we can predict his or her readiness (aptitude) for additional training in that subject and for jobs that require a knowledge of that subject.

The practical value of using tests to select and classify individuals in various educational and vocational contexts is that tests are the most economical and efficient means of identifying the individuals who are likely to be successful in given roles. As a matter of fact, the predictive validity of cognitive tests is what proponents of testing cite as the tests' most redeeming quality. Defenders of tests recognize that individuals from certain subpopulations typically achieve below-average scores, but they argue that the problem lies not with the tests but, rather, with the nation's schools, which fail to provide all young people with equal opportunities to develop the necessary skills.

> *Individuals from certain subpopulations typically achieve below-average [test] scores, but [supporters of these tests] argue that the problem lies not with the tests but, rather, with the nation's schools.*

The Pentagon's Study

In the summer of 1980 the Department of Defense and the military services, in cooperation with the Department of Labor, sponsored the project called *Profile of American Youth*, which was a large-scale research project designed to assess the vocational aptitudes of the contemporary American youth population. Its primary goal was to develop an aptitude profile of the current military-age population that the Department of Defense could use not only to evaluate the quality and representativeness of its new enlistees but also to plan for the future.[3]

Defense manpower analysts assess the quality of recruits according to two criteria: educational level and aptitude test scores.

Defense manpower analysts assess the quality of recruits according to two criteria: educational level and aptitude test scores. To determine the degree to which new recruits are qualitatively representative of the youth population as a whole, the analysts need data on the distribution of these characteristics in the civilian youth population. To obtain these data, the National Opinion Research Center of the University of Chicago, working under a contract with the Defense Department, administered the ASVAB to a statistically representative sample of American young people born between January 1, 1957, and December 31, 1964 (that is, people aged 16 through 23). Racially, the sample included 7,043 whites, 3,028 blacks, and 1,843 Hispanics.

The ASVAB includes 10 subtests: General Science, Arithmetic Reasoning, Word Knowledge, Paragraph Comprehension, Numerical Operations, Coding Speed, Auto and Shop Information, Mathematics Knowledge, Mechanical Comprehension, and Electronics Information. Most of the subtests require very specific factual knowledge; many of the skills assessed are the sort typically learned in school. Clearly, then, the primary purpose of the ASVAB is to survey developed abilities. But the abilities (levels of achievement) indicated by the test scores can then be used to predict subsequent performance. For example, a person who scores poorly on a basic arithmetic test probably has a poor aptitude for algebra.

The *Profile's* Findings

The results reported below apply to a *Profile* subsample of 9,173 young men and women 18 to 23 years of age (which is the primary age group from which the services recruit).[4] Included in the subsample are 5,533 whites, 2,298 blacks, and 1,342 Hispanics. The mean standard scores received on each of the 10 ASVAB subtests by the three racial/ethnic groups and by males and females within each group are presented in table 6-1. (The scores are set to a mean of 500 and a standard deviation of 100, which is the scale used to report SAT scores.) On each of the subtests, the differences in mean scores among the groups are considerable.*

Table 6-1 makes it clear that blacks will be particularly disadvantaged for any type of selection that relies on test performance as a criterion. This is true for tests that measure—

- the skills and knowledge typically thought to indicate scholastic aptitude;
- the basic literacy and numeracy skills; and
- specialized knowledge and technical skills.

On none of the tests do we observe parity in the performances of the three racial/ethnic groups.

The subtests that survey the skills and knowledge typically thought to indicate scholastic aptitude are arithmetic reasoning, word knowledge, numerical operations, paragraph comprehension, and mathematics knowledge. Differences between blacks and whites in performance on those subtests range from 133 points in word knowledge to 97 points in numerical operations. Performance on these subtests is highly dependent upon formal instruction and facility in the language of the dominant culture. Therefore, the relatively low quality of education that blacks and Hispanics receive in the public schools and their relative social isolation are strongly implicated in the differences in achievement among the racial or ethnic groups. Regardless of the reasons for the differences, however, the test data indicate that when test scores are used as a criterion for selection, blacks will be at a considerable disadvantage in the competition for higher educational placement.

The subtests that measure the basic literacy and

*Initially the Pentagon released the results in the form of percentile scores rather than standard scores, which may have caused some confusion. The mean percentile scores for the three major racial/ethnic groups were 56 for whites, 31 for Hispanics, and 24 for blacks. This does not mean, however, that the mean test score of blacks was less than half that of whites. A percentile score indicates the percentage of people who scored below the raw score obtained by the given individual. The best way for a lay reader to interpret the percentile scores is to say that 56 percent of whites scored "above average," that is, above the mean percentile of 50, whereas only 31 percent of Hispanics and 24 percent of blacks scored "above average."

*T*he test data indicate that when test scores are used as a criterion for selection, blacks will be at a considerable disadvantage in the competition for higher educational placement.

Table 6-1

ASVAB Subtest Mean Standard Scores of American Youth (18-23 Years), by Racial/Ethnic Group and Sex

Subtest	No. of Questions	Mean Standard Score								
		Male			Female			Total		
		White	Black	Hispanic	White	Black	Hispanic	White	Black	Hispanic
General science	25	543	405	438	501	393	400	522	399	419
Arithmetic reasoning	30	537	413	450	504	401	416	521	407	433
Word knowledge	35	524	386	429	525	397	416	525	392	423
Paragraph comprehension	15	510	399	427	530	422	431	520	411	429
Numerical operations	50	507	408	442	528	434	449	518	421	446
Coding speed	84	494	396	441	541	442	468	418	419	455
Auto and shop information	25	603	415	480	447	345	361	525	380	421
Mathematics knowledge	25	524	431	454	508	430	430	516	431	442
Mechanical comprehension	25	572	416	469	472	378	387	522	397	428
Electronics information	20	529	467	483	490	445	451	510	456	467

Source: M. J. Eitelberg and Z. D. Doering, "*Profile* in Perspective: The Policy and Research Implications of the *Profile of American Youth*," paper presented at the annual meeting of the American Psychological Association, Washington, D.C., August 24, 1982.

numeracy skills are word knowledge, paragraph comprehension, and numerical operations. Since those skills are indeed prerequisites for effective performance, even in low-skilled jobs, the scores portend problems for black youths in finding employment in jobs for which hiring decisions are based on test performance. The results of these subtests also confirm the relevance of concerns advanced by critics of the minimum competency testing movement. The adverse effects of these examinations fall disproportionately heavily on minority youths in general, and black youths in particular. When minimum competency tests are used as a requirement for high school graduation, a lower percentage of black 12th graders than white 12th graders will graduate.

The subtests that assess specialized knowledge and technical skills are mathematics knowledge, auto and shop information, mechanical comprehension, arithmetic reasoning, and electronics information. On these tests, the disparities among the performances of the three groups signal another kind of difficulty that blacks and Hispanics, in particular, face as they seek entry into the contemporary labor force and lucrative job placements. America's economy is increasingly technical, which gives the competitive advantage to individuals who enter the labor force with basic scientific and technical knowledge in addition to well-developed literacy and numeracy skills. In the technical areas, the test data suggest that blacks and Hispanics generally show skill levels too low to allow them to compete effectively with their white peers.

Although the greatest discrepancies in scoring appear among the three racial/ethnic groups, considerable differences in mean scores also appear between the sexes (table 6-1). The females in each of the racial/ethnic groups score considerably lower than their male counterparts in general science, arithmetic reasoning, mathematics knowledge, auto and shop information, mechanical comprehension, and electronics information. However, females in each of the groups perform better in numerical operations, coding speed, and paragraph comprehension; and black and white females score higher than their male counterparts in word knowledge. Among Hispanics, however, males score higher in word knowledge than females do. That is an interesting finding because differences in the development of verbal skills generally tend to favor females.

Essentially, the pattern of sex differences seen in the *Profile* study indicates that females have advan-

*A*merica's economy is increasingly technical, which gives the competitive advantage to individuals who enter the labor force with basic scientific and technical knowledge in addition to well-developed literacy and numeracy skills.

tages in the areas traditionally stereotyped as areas of female skill and that males have advantages in the areas stereotyped as areas of male skill. In other words, females are relatively disadvantaged for educational and vocational placements that require mathematical and technical skills and knowledge— placements, that is, in occupational areas in which females are currently underrepresented.

The study estimates that among white 18- to 23-year-olds, 16 percent have not completed high school; among blacks in the same age range, the percentage is twice as high: 32 percent.

In addition to providing information about scoring on standardized tests, the *Profile* study also looked at educational attainment, and in this respect, also, it reveals a difference among the racial/ethnic groups that is very important for their career prospects. The study estimates that among white 18- to 23-year-olds, 16 percent have not completed high school; among blacks in the same age range, the percentage is twice as high: 32 percent. Among Hispanics, although their performance in the ASVAB subtests exceeds that of blacks, 42 percent have not completed high school. Given the importance of a high school diploma for getting even the lowest skilled jobs, these differences in the rates at which youths finish high school reinforce the concerns often felt about the career prospects of very large segments of the black and Hispanic youth populations.

Test Scores and the Enlistment Eligibility of Black Youths

The significance of the *Profile* data as a barometer of the career prospects of black youths, particularly in contexts where selection and classification decisions are made on the basis of educational attainment and aptitude test scores, can be clearly demonstrated in the case of one long-standing equal opportunity employer: the military services.

The military's current operational criteria for determining "quality" in its recruiting are, as we know, educational attainment and entry-test scores. Those criteria grew out of the services' historical search for strategies to identify the "characteristics and attributes of military personnel that are considered desirable and that contribute to a more productive, capable, and better motivated force."[5]

In recruiting personnel to the enlisted ranks, the armed services place a high premium on completion of high school. This emphasis is the result of years of experience which indicate that "a person who did not graduate from high school is twice as likely to leave the military before completing the first three years of service as a high school diploma graduate."[6]

To determine an applicant's "trainability" in the military services, the military administers the ASVAB.* Scores on four of the ASVAB subtests (word knowledge, paragraph comprehension, arithmetic reasoning, and numerical operations) are combined to produce the Armed Forces Qualifying Test (AFQT) score, which is a primary criterion for enlistment into the armed services. Various other ASVAB subtest composites are used to make military job training assignments.

The aptitude composites commonly used are—

- *mechanical* (mechanical comprehension + auto and shop information + general science subtests);

- *administrative* (coding speed + numerical operations + paragraph comprehension + word knowledge subtests);

- *general* (arithmetic reasoning + paragraph comprehension + word knowledge subtests); and

- *electronics* (arithmetic reasoning + electron ics information + general science + mathematics knowledge subtests).

Racial-Ethnic and Sex Differences in Enlistment Eligibility

Scores on the AFQT have traditionally been organized in terms of percentile scores and grouped into five broad categories. The percentile-score ranges for each of the five categories are as follows:

"A person who did not graduate from high school is twice as likely to leave the military before completing the first three years of service as a high school diploma graduate."

---

*The first large-scale standardized testing in the United States began during World War I. Since that time, the armed services have invested a considerable amount of effort in developing reliable and valid methods to screen persons before they enter military service.

AFQT Category	Percentile Score Range
I	93-100
II	65-92
III	31-64
IV	10-30
V	1-9

People who score in categories I and II are viewed as above average in trainability; in category III, average; in category IV, below average; and in category V, markedly below average and, under current service policy, ineligible for enlistment.[7]

Table 6-2 shows the distribution by AFQT category and racial/ethnic group for two classes of youths: the 1980 youth population sampled in the *Profile* and the 1981 recruits who had not had previous service experience. With respect to the "representative quality" of the FY 1981 recruits, the data speak well for the all-volunteer force. As the test scores indicate, the services are attracting capable young people. Although white youths who score in the above-average trainability categories are not enlisting in quite the same proportions as they are represented in the 1980 youth population, 86 percent of those who enlisted achieved scores in the average range or better (total of columns I, II, and III in the row denoting total DOD white accessions). In the case of black youths, the services recruited a higher percentage of average or better scorers than occurs in the black youth population as a whole.

However, the data also indicate that a large segment of the black youth population will have problems qualifying for military service. Whereas almost half the white youths in the 1980 population (44 percent) obtained test scores that would place them in the two above-average trainability categories, only 7 percent of black youths obtained scores that would place them in those same two categories—and 72 percent socred in categories IV and V. Since current policies limit the percentage of recruits from category IV to 20 percent and prohibit the enlistment of recruits from category V, many black youths who may wish to enlist in the armed services do not qualify.

In the case of black youths, the services recruited a higher percentage of average or better scorers than occurs in the black youth population as a whole.

Table 6-2

Distribution of 1980 Youth Population and FY 1981 Non-Prior-Service Accessions, by Armed Forces Qualifications Test (AFQT) Category and Racial/Ethnic Group

Racial/Ethnic Group and Population Group	AFQT Category						AFQT 50 or above
	I	II	III	IV	V	Total	
			(Percent)				(Percent)
White							
1980 Youth	5	39	34	19	3	100	61
FY 1981 Accessions							
Army	3	27	46	24	0	100	48
Navy	4	38	48	20	0	100	66
Marine Corps	3	35	52	10	0	100	63
Air Force	4	42	47	7	0	100	71
Total DOD	3	35	48	14	0	100	61
Black							
1980 Youth	0	7	21	46	26	100	14
FY 1981 Accessions							
Army	0	5	34	61	0	100	13
Navy	0	11	49	40	0	100	26
Marine Corps	0	11	57	32	0	100	30
Air Force	1	17	67	15	0	100	44
Total DOD	0	9	46	45	0	100	23
Hispanic							
1980 Youth	1	13	27	39	20	100	23
FY 1981 Accessions							
Army	0	7	38	55	0	100	18
Navy	1	21	53	25	0	100	42
Marine Corps	1	13	63	23	0	100	37
Air Force	0	24	64	12	0	100	52
Total DOD	1	14	50	35	0	100	33

Source: Office of the Assistant Secretary of Defense, *Profile of American Youth*, p. 24.

Indeed, analyses performed by the Brookings Institution support that conclusion (table 6-3). Using the enlistment standards in effect in the four service branches during FY 1981, Martin Binkin and his co-authors estimated the percentage of American youths of military age who would qualify for military service, given their distribution of educational level

65

and aptitude socres.[8] These projections make clear the considerable advantage enjoyed by white youths for enlistment in all services, compared with both black and Hispanic youths—even when the groups are similar in educational attainment. Among black youths who meet educational attainment standards— that is, who have a high school diploma—their lower average test performance considerably undermines their potential for enlistment.

This suggests that the public education system does not provide equal opportunities for all young people to develop adequate labor market skills. Discrepancies among young people from different groups who have spent the same amount of time in school and earned similar credentials were documented more than two decades ago;[9] the data from the Pentagon's *Profile* study suggest that the situation has not changed much since that time.

The mean AFQT scores of the 1980 youth population by sex, racial/ethnic group, and educational level are displayed in table 6-4. It is apparent that the performance of individuals in each racial/ethnic group increases with education, although at each educational level there is a substantial gap favoring white youths. It is interesting to note that the difference in achievement between black males and white males is smaller when the individuals being measured do not have high school diplomas (102 points) than when they do (133 points). The same is not true of black and white females. These data suggest that education does more to close the performance gap between white and black females than it does to close the gap between white and black males. Why this is the case cannot be determined from these descriptive data, but the trend clearly deserves more attention in view of the difficulty black males experience in competing for jobs.

It is also rather peculiar that among black males, and only among black males, individuals who hold the General Educational Development Certificate (GED) have higher average AFQT scores than do their peers with high school diplomas. Of course, this unexpected finding may be attributable to the small number of black males in the sample who have the GED credential (N = 49), which would result in an

*[T*he Pentagon's Profile *study] suggests that education does more to close the performance gap between white and black females than it does to close the gap between white and black males.*

Table 6-3

Estimated Percentage of American Youths (18-23 Years) Who Would Qualify for Enlistment in the Military Service, by Racial/Ethnic Group and Educational Level

Racial/Ethnic Group and Education	Military Service Branch			
	Army	Navy	Marine Corps	Air Force
White				
Non-high-school graduate	41.7	19.9	22.5	11.2
GED equivalency	76.0	70.4	35.1	56.1
High school graduate	96.4	87.5	79.8	85.1
Total	85.7	74.5	67.7	70.5
Black				
Non-high-school graduate	7.1	3.8	3.0	0.8
GED equivalency	35.2	26.6	13.9	11.2
High school graduate	68.6	45.6	33.8	32.1
Total	48.1	31.7	23.6	21.5
Hispanic				
Non-high-school graduate	13.6	4.8	5.5	1.5
GED equivalency	40.0	35.7	18.8	16.8
High school graduate	85.7	64.8	54.7	56.7
Total	54.6	39.2	33.3	32.7
All Groups				
Non-high-school graduate	31.6	15.0	16.8	8.0
GED	68.0	62.1	31.1	47.4
High school graduate	92.7	81.6	73.2	77.6
Total	78.7	66.6	59.6	61.5

Note: Estimates of the percentages of youths qualified for military service were calculated on the basis of results from the *Profile of American Youth* administration of the Armed Services Vocational Aptitude Battery (ASVAB) to a national probability sample in 1980 and the 1981 education/aptitude standards used by the armed services. It should be noted that eligibility for enlistment would also depend on other factors, including medical and moral requirements.

Source: Binkin et al., *Blacks and the Military*, p. 98, and special tabulations provided by the Office of the Assistant Secretary of Defense for Manpower, Reserve Affairs, and Logistics.

Table 6-4

Mean AFQT Standard Scores of American Youths (18-23 Years), by Sex, Racial/Ethnic Group, and Educational Level

Racial/Ethnic Group and Sex	Non-High-School Graduate	GED High School Equivalency	High School Graduate and Above
White			
Male	467	518	550
Female	468	517	543
Total	468	517	547
Black			
Male	365	436	417
Female	346	441	456
Total	356	439	438
Hispanic			
Male	388	470	505
Female	392	447	484
Total	392	460	494
All Groups			
Male	446	502	540
Female	446	500	529
Total	446	501	533

Source: M. J. Eitelberg and Z. D. Doering, "*Profile* in Perspective: The Policy and Research Implications of the *Profile of American Youth*," paper presented at the annual meeting of the American Psychological Association, Washington, D.C., August 24, 1982.

unreliable statistical comparison. Black female GED holders included in the sample are even fewer in number (N = 24), but they score lower than their counterparts with high school diplomas.

Despite the gaps in performance among the racial/ethnic groups at each educational level, then, education clearly makes a substantial difference in the performance of all young people. Generally speaking, test scores rise with the number of years of schooling completed. This finding attests to the role that education can play in raising the skill levels of individuals and thus in allowing them to compete more effectively for educational and vocational placements.

Regional Differences in Enlistment Eligibility

The average AFQT scores of young people in various regions of the country by sex and racial/ethnic group are displayed in table 6-5. Young people in the South generally score lower than their peers in other regions, and blacks in the South generally score lower than either their white counterparts in that region or blacks in other regions of the country. Perhaps it should be expected that the lowest performance seen for both whites and blacks would occur in the South, since several states in that region (such as Alabama, Arkansas, Mississippi, Tennessee, and Georgia) rank among the lowest in per pupil expenditure for education. In contrast, the highest scores occur in the northeast and north central regions, which include states that rank among the highest in per pupil expenditure (for example, New York, New Jersey, Michigan, and Illinois).[10] Apparently the extent to which states are willing to invest in education is reflected in the achievement of their young people. If this is the case, the regional differences seen here in skill development may become more pronounced, because current federal policy toward education has reversed past federal efforts to equalize educational spending.

Although youths in the Northeast generally show a scoring advantage over their peers in other regions of the country, the data in table 6-5 suggest that this is attributable primarily to the high scores of whites in that region. The average scores of blacks in the region are not considerably higher than those of their peers in other regions and are actually lower than the average for blacks in the West. The educational or other resources that account for the superior performance of whites in the Northeast do not extend to the black population in the same region. This may be related to the fact that the states in the Northeast with the largest percentages of black youths (New York, New Jersey, and Pennsylvania) also have considerable racial/ethnic segregation of students in the public schools.[11]

Blacks in the South generally score lower than either their white counterparts in that region or blacks in other regions of the country.

Career Prospects of Black Youths

Because of their relatively low aptitude scores, black young people who qualify for enlistment can be expected to find poorer training opportunities and career prospects in the military. Support for this projection is given in table 6-6, which displays the average composite scores of whites, blacks, and Hispanics in the occupational areas typically used by the military services. High scores on the mechanical and electronics composites are usually a prerequisite for training in technical skills—training that is likely to allow someone to advance in the military or to compete for a good job in the civilian labor force. As the table shows, on the basis of their composite scores very few blacks are likely to qualify for training in technical skills. Instead, black youths are more likely to be assigned to "soft, non-technical skills where training is minimal and advancement is slow."[12]

The failure of black youths to qualify for technical training in the military means that military service is not likely to alter substantially their vocational prospects in the civilian labor force. This may help to explain why the unemployment rates for black veterans are consistently higher than those of white veterans and are not significantly different from the unemployment rates for comparably aged black males who have never served in the military.[13] The high reenlistment rates of blacks may also be attributable to the kind of training they receive in the military. Without the skills to get a good job, or, indeed, any job in the civilian labor force, young blacks may well decide that leaving the military is impractical.

Summary and Conclusion

The relatively low performance of black young people on the military enlistment test has a significant effect on their career prospects in the military. In other contexts where test scores are used as criteria for selection and classification, we can expect black young people to have comparably low scores, with similar effects on their prospects. The use of test scores continues to be a prominent feature of American society, despite public concern about the fairness of the practice, and the poor test performance of

> *B*ecause of their relatively low aptitude scores, black young people who qualify for enlistment can be expected to find poorer training opportunities and career prospects in the military.

Table 6-5

Mean AFQT Standard Scores of American Youths (18-23 Years), by Sex, Racial/ Ethnic Group, and Geographic Region

Racial/Ethnic Group and Sex	Northeast	North Central	South	West
White				
Male	534	530	508	521
Female	534	520	510	527
Total	534	526	509	524
Black				
Male	406	425	382	410
Female	422	397	402	426
Total	412	410	392	417
Hispanic				
Male	420	428	457	428
Female	388	436	430	429
Total	405	432	443	429
All Groups				
Male	512	520	477	500
Female	512	507	479	505
Total	512	514	479	503

Source: Eitelberg and Doering, "*Profile* in Perspective."

Table 6-6

Mean ASVAB Composite Scores for the 1980 Youth Population, by Racial/Ethnic Group

ASVAB Composite	White (N = 5,533)	Black (N = 2,298)	Hispanic (N = 1,342)
Mechanical	522	401	431
Administrative	521	406	438
General	522	402	429
Electronics	521	407	428

Source: J. H. Laurence, M. J. Eitelberg, and B. K. Waters, "Subpopulation Analyses of 1980 Youth Population Aptitudes," paper presented at the annual meeting of the American Psychological Association, Washington, D.C., August 24, 1982.

black youths can therefore be expected to depress considerably their future educational and vocational opportunities.

The data from the *Profile* study raise two important questions: why are the disparities in the test performances of black, Hispanic, and white youths so great, and what can be done to decrease, if not eliminate, those disparities? In our search for answers to these questions, it is clear that we must focus our attention on the nation's system of public education.

Endnotes

1. M. L. Tenopyr, "The Realities of Employment Testing," *American Psychologist* 36:1120-27.

2. A. Anastasi, *Psychological Testing,* 5th ed. (New York: Macmillan, 1982).

3. W. S. Sellman and Z. D. Doering, "The Profile of American Youth: Background and Description of the 1980 Nationwide Administration of the Armed Services Vocational Aptitude Battery," paper presented at the Annual Meeting of the American Psychological Association, Washington, D.C., August 24, 1982.

4. According to the Department of Defense, the results for 16- and 17-year-old youths are similar to those for the older youths. Office of the Assistant Secretary of Defense for Manpower, Reserve Affairs and Logistics, *Profile of American Youth: 1980 Nationwide Administration of the Armed Services Vocational Aptitude Battery* (Washington, D.C.: Department of Defense, 1982), p. 11.

5. Z. D. Doering, M. J. Eitelberg, and W. S. Sellman, "Uniforms and Jeans: A Comparison of the 1981 Military Recruits With the 1980 Youth Population," paper presented at the Annual Meeting of the American Psychological Association, Washington, D.C., August 24, 1982, p. 2.

6. *Profile,* p. 19.

7. *Profile,* Table 3, p.7.

8. M. Binkin and M. J. Eitelberg with A. J. Schexnider and M. M. Smith, *Blacks and the Military* (Washington, D.C.: The Brookings Institution, 1982).

9. J. S. Coleman, E. Q. Campbell, C. J. Hobson, J. McPartland, A. M. Moody, F. D. Weinfeld, and R. L. York, *Equality of Educational Opportunity* (Washington, D.C.: GPO, 1966).

10. W. V. Grant and L. J. Eiden, *Digest of Education Statistics* (Washington, D.C.: National Center for Education Statistics, 1982).

11. G. Orfield, *School Desegregation Patterns in the States, Large Cities, and Metropolitan Areas, 1968-1980* (Washington, D.C.: Joint Center for Political Studies, 1983).

12. Binkin et al., *Blacks and the Military,* p. 55.

13. *Employment and Training Report of the President* (Washington, D.C.: GPO, 1981).

7. THE ALL-VOLUNTEER FORCE AND THE MARKETPLACE

Charles C. Moskos

T hen there is the troublesome issue of racial imbalance. Just as was the case during the Vietnam era, blacks and other minorities still comprise a much greater percentage of the Armed Forces than they do of the general population. This is especially so in the combat forces. To many, that is an undemocratic situation. An army whose soldiers come disproportionately from disadvantaged groups—whether voluntarily or not—violates our sense of fairness.[1]

Since 1977, the United States has sought to accomplish something it has never attempted before: to maintain more than two million persons on active military duty, along with an expanded reserve force, on a completely voluntary basis. The aspect of the all-volunteer force that has generated more discussion than any other is the racial representativeness of those who join the armed forces. This is reflected in the above quote from Ford Foundation President Franklin Thomas. But in fact, as I shall explain, the issue of race is intertwined with, and ultimately subordinate to, issues of social class—issues that reflect a shift in the basis of military service and involve questions of military effectiveness. Moreover, the reason that those particular issues of social class have arisen is that the country's military recruitment policy is grounded on marketplace principles. I claim, therefore, that by focusing on the racial composition of the military, analysts deflect attention from the central issue: should primary reliance for staffing the all-volunteer force be placed upon supply and demand variables in the labor force?

The issue of race is intertwined with, and ultimately subordinate to, issues of social class.

The basis of the current all-volunteer system was established by the 1970 Gates Commission Report. The report was founded on a marketplace philosophy,[2] and during all presidential administrations since then, the terminology of econometric analysis, with its aura of precision, has been the common coin of discussions of military manpower policy. Founding a recruitment philosophy on supply and demand variables, or marketplace principles, has meant shifting the basis of military service. The obligations of citizenship have been replaced by the forces of laissez-faire economics. Instead of being drawn to military service by their sense of civic duty, citizens have been led to look on military service as a way of finding employment when all other ways seem closed.

It is not surprising, therefore, to find that a shift has also taken place in the social-class bases of the lower enlisted ranks, especially in the army. Middle-class Americans are increasingly underrepresented; lower-class Americans are increasingly overrepresented. And that shift, which cuts across the races, not only operates to the disadvantage of the poverty youths themselves but also impairs military effectiveness. (Evidence exists that a military whose combat arms are staffed by a cross section of American youths is stronger than a military whose combat arms are staffed mainly by the underprivileged and undereducated.)

Evidence exists that a military whose combat arms are staffed by a cross section of American youths is stronger than a military whose combat arms are staffed mainly by the underprivileged and undereducated.

To most proponents of the all-volunteer force, however, the consequences of a marketplace philosophy for the ideal of citizen obligation and for military effectiveness are secondary considerations. Leaders of the black community by and large approve of the redefinition of military service, primarily because the armed forces can offer employment to large numbers of black youths. And affluent white Americans are pleased that their sons are no longer being drafted. In contrast, my contention is that citizen obligation and military effectiveness are precisely the contexts within which the racial and social transformations of the armed forces must be placed—and, as a result, we must question the value of a marketplace philosophy.

My attention will be mainly on the army, the largest of the services, the one that relied most

76

heavily on the draft and that is most often regarded as the bellwether of the all-volunteer force.

Race and Class in the Army

Despite some legerdemain in its presentation of official statistics, the Department of Defense has provided conclusive evidence that during the first decade of the all-volunteer force, the enlisted ranks of the army were much less racially representative of American male youths than were the military ranks during the peacetime draft. Black participation in the army had begun increasing even before the advent of the all-volunteer force; and between 1973 and 1982, the percentage of black entrants almost tripled over pre-Vietnam levels. The rising percentage of blacks could be attributed, at least in part, to the substantial rise in the number of blacks eligible for military service—most notably, the rise in the number of blacks who were high school graduates. Another contributing factor was the combined push of the astoundingly high unemployment rate among black youths and the pull of an institution that has perhaps gone further than any other to attack racism.[3]

The Pentagon's picture of the racial composition of recruits, however, represents a decade-long view and ignores the fluctuations of atypical good or bad recruitment years within the decade. More specifically, the Pentagon's picture ignores the relationship between recruitment and the state of the economy—an omission that stretches credulity.

Although the percentage of black entrants into military service rose during the late 1970s, in the early 1980s—when the economy declined—the percentage of blacks entering the military declined as well. In 1979, blacks made up 36 percent of army entrants; in 1983, the corresponding figure was 23 percent. In brief, bad economic times brought more white recruits.

More to the point is that both the disproportionately high black entrant rate in the late 1970s and the drop in that rate in the early 1980s were accompanied by a shift in the class distribution of recruits, in relation to class distribution during the peacetime draft. For example:

Citizen obligation and military effectiveness are precisely the contexts within which the racial and social transformations of the armed forces must be placed—and, as a result, we must question the value of a marketplace philosophy.

77

Today the army's enlisted ranks are the only major segment of American society where the educational levels of blacks surpass those of whites.

- In the 10 years after the end of the draft, al most one recruit in 20 had some college education; the comparable figure for the 10 years before the Vietnam War was more than one recruit in five.

- In the 10 years after the end of the draft, 66 percent of black male recruits and 58 percent of white male recruits had a high school diploma. In the civilian population for the same period and the equivalent age group, about 70 percent of black males and 80 percent of white males were high school graduates.

- During the first decade of the all-volunteer force, only about one in three male recruits was a white high school graduate.

An especially noteworthy statistic is the intersection of race and education. Among male entrants in the all-volunteer army (among female entrants, as well—see below), that intersection is quite different from what it is in the country as a whole. Nationwide, the educational levels of blacks have trailed behind those of whites; but since the end of the draft, the percentage of black high school graduates entering the army has consistently exceeded that of whites. Thus, today the army's enlisted ranks are the only major segment of American society where the educational levels of blacks surpass those of whites.

This reflects in part the reality that white high school dropouts tend to score higher on entrance tests than black high school dropouts and are therefore more likely to be accepted into the army.* More important, it represents the fact that among all high school graduates, blacks are more than twice as likely as whites to enter the military; and among qualified youths, black high school graduates are three times more likely than white high school graduates to join the military.[4]

---

*Among all high school dropouts during the era of the all-volunteer force, an estimated 16.6 percent of whites and 12.1 percent of blacks entered the military. Among those high school dropouts who were qualified for military service, however, blacks were three times more likely to enter the military than whites. Binkin et al., *Blacks and the Military,* p. 66.

78

So what has happened in the all-volunteer army, I suggest, is something like the following: whereas the black soldier has been fairly representative of the black community in terms of educational background, white entrants, especially before 1980, have been coming from the least educated sectors of the white community. In other words, the all-volunteer army has attracted not only a disproportionate number of minorities, but also a segment of white youths that, in educational (or social) terms, is unrepresentative. These young whites are, if anything, even more uncharacteristic of the broader social mix than are our minority soldiers. Though put far too crassly, an insight was given to me by a long-time German employee of the U.S. Army in Europe: "In the volunteer army you are recruiting the best of the blacks and the worst of the whites."

Resocialization

There is nothing new in the military's recruiting large numbers of youths—white, black, and brown—who have no real alternative job prospects. It has always done so and will always continue to do so. Moreover, the military will continue to draw disproportionately on young blacks as long as they are victims of certain structural defects in the national economy—specifically, the steady flow of manufacturing jobs away from cities where so many poor blacks are trapped. But current tendencies to label the army as a recourse for America's underclasses *are* new—and they do a disservice to the youths involved, precisely because those tendencies run directly counter to the premise that military participation is a matter of broad-based national service.

That premise was essential to the military's role during the peacetime draft, from the 1950s through the mid-1960s, in serving as a bridging environment for low-status youths who hoped eventually to gain stable employment.[5] The fact that the armed forces were legitimated on grounds other than overt welfare—grounds such as national defense, citizenship obligation, patriotism, even manly honor—was the basis for whatever success the military had as a remedial organization for deprived youths.[6] In other words, the conditions peculiar to the armed forces

Though put far too crassly, an insight was given by a long-time German employee of the U.S. Army in Europe: "In the volunteer army you are recruiting the best of the blacks and the worst of the whites."

79

that serve to resocialize poverty youths toward productive ends depend directly upon the military's not being perceived as an employer of last resort. But unless enlisted membership reflects a cross section of American youth, the army will find it increasingly difficult to avoid such a characterization, even if unfair.

The fact that the disproportionately white navy and the racially balanced air force have also had problems recruiting from the middle class during the all-volunteer era indicates that something besides racial composition is at work.

The barrier to attracting a cross section of youths is broader than the army's changing racial composition, although surely white reluctance to join an increasingly black organization is a factor. But I am unpersuaded that even if the army were overwhelmingly white, any significant number of middle-class whites—or middle-class people of any race, for that matter—would be likely to join the army, *given current recruitment incentives.* The fact that the disproportionately white navy and the racially balanced air force have also had problems recruiting from the middle class during the all-volunteer era indicates that something besides racial composition is at work. Moreover, the sharp rise in white army entrants in the early 1980s suggests that any tipping effect toward blacks can be reversed by economic hard times.

Military Effectiveness

The metamorphosis in the racial and social representativeness of army recruits is, in the long run, not good for the recruits themselves. And the question also arises as to whether it has been good, bad, or indifferent for military effectiveness. Two measures of military effectiveness are attrition from the enlisted ranks and the composition of the combat arms.

Attrition Rates

Attrition can come about in one of two ways: premature discharge and regular separation (refusal to reenlist). Defense manpower analysts, however, focus on aggregate turnover rates; thus, they obscure the fundamental difference between the two kinds of attrition. Yet, the differences between recruits who are prematurely discharged and recruits who make regular separations from the military have tremendous implications for military effectiveness and command climate.

In the dominant econometric model of the all-volunteer force, it is mistakenly assumed that long initial enlistments are always to be preferred over short enlistments. From that point of view, the all-volunteer force has done much better than the peacetime draft. In 1980, 61 percent of all enlisted entrants signed on for four or more years, compared with 36 percent in 1964. Yet, because the all-volunteer force has problems of retention (reenlistment) and a high attrition rate from premature discharges, personnel turnover has been about the same as during the peacetime draft era.

Problems of retention are caused by the army's structure of compensation. The principal attraction used to induce people to join the all-volunteer force was large increases in military pay for lower ranked enlisted personnel. (For example, in 1983 a private first class living off-base received close to $15,000 a year in salary and benefits.) But that front-loading of compensation toward the junior ranks dramatically compressed the pay scales of the career enlisted force, and problems of retention followed.

Premature discharges, which have also been a problem since the end of conscription, have involved about one in three service members. Put another way, since 1973 more than 800,000 young people have been discharged from the military before completing their initial term of enlistment, for reasons of indiscipline, personality disorders, job ineptitude, and the like. The attrition rate from premature discharges has been especially high in the combat arms and labor-intensive positions. The striking finding about premature discharges is that high school dropouts are twice as likely as high school graduates to leave the military without completing their enlistments (see table 7-1). This finding remains virtually unchanged when mental group level is held constant. Possession of a high school diploma, it seems, reflects the acquisition of traits (good work habits, perseverance, punctuality) that make for a more successful military experience. Studies of unauthorized absences and desertions show that such behavior is most likely to occur among those with the least education, those

High school dropouts are twice as likely as high school graduates to leave the military without completing their enlistments.

Table 7-1

Premature Discharge of 1979 Army Male Entrants Within Two Years of Enlistment, by Race, Mental Group, and Level of Education

	White Percentage	Black Percentage
High school graduates		
Mental group		
I-IIIA	21.4	20.9
IIIB	24.7	19.9
IV	29.6	19.6
All graduates	23.2	20.2
Non-high-school graduates		
Mental group		
I-IIIA	44.9	39.3
IIIB	48.2	40.4
IV	42.7	31.6
All non-graduates	46.8	40.1
Total Army	33.8	26.9

from broken homes, and those who were in trouble with the law before entering the service. The evidence further shows that, on measures of productivity, soldiers with more education do better across the board, in low-skilled as well as in high-skilled jobs.[7]

Partly because black recruits are more likely than white recruits to be high school graduates, black soldiers have a lower rate of premature discharge than do white soldiers. But even when education is held constant, blacks are slightly more likely to complete their enlistments than their white counterparts are. In point of fact, at every level of mental group and education, blacks have lower rates of premature discharge than whites. Even more revealing, as table 7-1 also shows, blacks placing in the lowest levels of the mental test distribution have rates of premature discharge significantly lower than whites in the same mental group levels. Certainly this evidence suggests, at the least, that motivational factors can

Table 7-2

Premature Discharge of 1979 Army Female Entrants Within Two Years of Enlistment, by Race and Mental Group (High School Graduates)

	White Percentage	Black Percentage
Mental Group		
I-IIIA	45.2	31.1
IIIB	47.3	31.9
IV	68.2	30.8
Total Army	45.6	31.4

override presumed aptitude differences in predicting completion of an enlistment. The data also show that mental test scores are in general much less effective predictors of premature-discharge rates for blacks than for whites.[8]

Among women, the same picture emerges, and even more strikingly so (see table 7-2). Not only has the percentage of black female recruits to the army increased in recent years, but the percentage also exceeds the percentage of black male recruits. Between 1979 and 1982, blacks accounted for close to four in 10 female entrants. And black females are much more likely to complete their enlistments than are white females. Inasmuch as nearly all female recruits enter with high school diplomas, no educational controls can be applied, but when mental group level is held constant, the lower premature-discharge rates of black females becomes even more marked. The significant differences in premature discharges between black and white females is noteworthy and deserves study.

The Combat Arms

The second measure of military effectiveness is combat effectiveness. And even though the behavior of soldiers in the ultimate test of combat cannot be calculated precisely, most military professionals believe that combat effectiveness improves if the

Table 7-3

First-Term Army Enlisted Personnel in Combat Arms, by Education and Race, 1980

	Total	White	Black
Non-high-school graduates	36.0%	37.4%	33.0%
High school graduates	26.9	27.1	24.9

combatants include soldiers who are better educated and more intelligent. Historical evidence supports that view.

Being educated or from the middle class does not make one braver or more able; but the chemistry of unit cohesion improves when a unit's members have a variety of talents and backgrounds and feel a sense of commitment to their group and to the larger society. Commanders and NCOs who remember the draft period have observed that middle-class and upwardly mobile youths enriched both the skill level and the commitment of military units in peace as well as in war. Research evidence confirms those observations. In addition, studies of combat soldiers in World War II and the Korean War show that soldiers with more education and higher mental scores were rated as better fighters by peers and immediate superiors.[9] Whatever scholarly debates may occur about performance indicators, the judgment of members of combat groups by other members is probably the most valid performance measure possible.

The soldiers of the all-volunteer force have not been put to the ultimate test of combat, but the findings of survey researchers on one essential component of combat effectiveness—disaffection— are discomfiting. A comparison of survey data collected from volunteer soldiers in the 1970s and from various groups serving in World War II is revealing. Peacetime all-volunteer-force soldiers were more disaffected than combat soldiers in World War II (who were more disaffected than the support

THE FINE IS:

$10.00

FOR BOOKS RETURNED
AFTER THE DATE
STAMPED IN THE BOOK

troops of that war). The level of disaffection in the all-volunteer force came closest to the level of the most disaffected group in World War II samples--a unit of military prisoners![10]

In an extensive survey of youths in America in 1979, the alienation levels of army enlisted men exceeded, by a significant margin, the alienation levels of all other comparison groups, including unemployed youths.[11] Another survey concluded that the all-volunteer force was drawing soldiers from the most socially alienated segment of the youth population. That conclusion raises questions about soldierly effectiveness in the event of hostilities.[12]

The social composition of the combat arms in 1980 is conveyed by table 7-3, which shows the likelihood that soldiers of certain racial and educational backgrounds will be assigned to the combat arms. The likelihood of a combat arms assignment is greater for a high school dropout (36.0 percent) than for a high school graduate (26.9 percent). This is not particularly surprising; but it is somewhat surprising to find that among soldiers at a similar educational level, whites are slightly more likely than blacks to be assigned to the combat arms. (From a historical standpoint, the evidence is clear that military participation and combat risks were more equally shared among American men of whatever race and class during World War II than during either the Korean or the Vietnam wars. Thus, in and of itself, the draft is no guarantee of class equity.)

In the event of hostilities, the racial composition of the combat arms will take on special significance. It would be naive, if not duplicitous, to state that disproportionately high black casualties would have no or only minor consequences on the domestic political scene. During the Vietnam War, controversies surrounded high black casualty rates despite the fact that black casualties *in toto* were not disproportionate to the black percentage of the American population (see table 7-4). Black casualty rates were highest in the early years of the Vietnam War, constituting about 20 percent of all casualties during 1965-67, but black protest against the war became, if anything, even more pronounced after 1967. In light of the Vietnam experience, we can expect outrage in the event

In an extensive survey of youths in America in 1979, the alienation levels of army enlisted men exceeded, by a significant margin, the alienation levels of all other comparison groups, including unemployed youths.

85

Table 7-4
Combat Deaths in Southeast Asia, 1964-1974

	Officer		Enlisted		Total	
	% Black	No. All Races	% Black	No. All Races	% Black	No. All Races
Army	2.7	3,393	14.2	27,470	12.5	30,863
Marine Corps	0.6	785	13.0	12,274	12.3	13,059
Air Force	1.1	1,284	8.1	394	2.9	1,678
Navy	0.5	385	0.3	1,208	0.3	1,593
All services	1.9	5,847	13.5	41,346	12.1	47,193

Source: Department of Defense.

minority casualties were to range from 30 to 40 percent of the total.* (Studies of Vietnam War casualties have documented that low social class, and not race per se, was the grouping most strongly correlated with the high casualties suffered by Americans in that war.[13])

Table 7-5 lists the percentage of army enlisted personnel, by race, in the combat arms for the years 1945, 1962, 1970, and 1980. In 1962 and 1970, blacks were at least twice as heavily represented in the combat arms as they were in the total army, but by 1980 the percentage of blacks assigned to combat roles was less than the percentage of blacks in the total army. It is to be stressed, however, that blacks in 1980 were still disproportionately concentrated in the combat arms in terms of their numbers in American society, if not in terms of their percentage in the army.

If U.S. forces are to fulfill their function of military deterrence in the post-Vietnam period, representational concerns are still germane. As is shown in table 7-6, there can be no question that

---

*Although casualties among poor whites would probably be proportionately even higher, the political ramifications would probably be more muted. My reasoning is that poor whites are less of an organized collectivity than blacks and their interests are less likely to be articulated by an intelligentsia or the media.

Table 7-5

Army Enlisted Personnel in Combat Arms, Selected Years, by Race

	1945	1962	1970	1980
Percentage of total personnel in combat arms	44.5%	26.0%	23.8%	26.4%
Percentage of total white personnel in combat arms	48.2	24.9	23.4	26.6
Percentage of total black personnel in combat arms	12.1	33.4	26.0	25.1
Blacks as percentage of total personnel	10.5	12.1	13.5	32.6

defining military service in economic rather than citizenship terms led to an unrepresentative enlisted force in the all-volunteer army, at least until the recruitment picture changed in the early 1980s.

In this regard, casualties in combat units in the post-Vietnam era are revealing. For the 237 people killed in the 1983 bombing of the marine barracks in Beirut, the racial distribution was whites 75 percent, blacks 22 percent, and others 3 percent. For the 248 soldiers of the 101st Airborne (Air Assault) Division killed in the 1985 airplane crash in Gander, Newfoundland, the racial breakdown was whites 77 percent, blacks 20 percent, and others 3 percent.

Policy Considerations

Difficulties in sustaining a volunteer force always lead to renewed talk of restoring conscription. Conscription, though, would have several problems. First, a return to the draft would pose anew the question of who should serve when most do not serve. During the peacetime draft of the 1950s, when the military was large and the youth cohort—the group of maturing Depression babies—was small, about three-quarters of the eligible men served in the

Table 7-6

Educational Levels of Male Youth Population, Total Army and Army Combat Branches, by Race, 1980

	% Of Whites	% Of Blacks
Male youth population (18-21 years)[a]		
Some college	36.2	23.6
High school graduate	45.6	45.7
Non-high-school graduate	18.2	30.7
(N in thousands)	(6,480)	(843)
Total army (first termers)		
Some college	4.1	3.5
High school graduate	57.3	68.0
Non-high-school graduate	38.6	28.5
(N in thousands)	(198)	(117)
Army combat arms (first termers)		
Some college	2.1	1.6
High school graduate	49.9	62.3
Non-high-school graduate	48.0	36.1
(N in thousands)	(64)	(32)

[a]Excludes those still enrolled in high school.

Source: U.S. Bureau of the Census, *Current Population Reports,* School Enrollment—Social and Economic Characteristics of Students, series P-20, no. 362, issued May 1981.

military.[14] The proportion of men drafted in the 1950s was even higher than the proportion drafted during the Vietnam War. Now, however, if manpower needs remain at current levels, only about one in four eligible males would be drafted or would otherwise serve in the military.* Since, among qualified male youths, an estimated 14 percent of whites and 42 percent of blacks have entered the military during the era of the all-volunteer force,[15] any draft system probably would curtail the number of black entrants.

---

*By 1990, to maintain current force levels (both active and reserve), one of every four males will be required to enter the military, one of every three qualified males, and one of every two qualified males not enrolled in college.

Second, to have a workable conscription requires a national consensus, especially within the relevant youth population, as to the need for conscription. Such a consensus does not exist currently and seems unlikely in the foreseeable future. Induction would probably lead to turbulence on many college campuses. Moreover, if compulsion were used, many would attempt to avoid military service, which would cause other problems. Even under a seemingly fair lottery system, decisions would have to be made that would erode the fairness of the induction process. That there seemed to be no practical way to handle the estimated half-million nonregistrants in 1982 does not give one confidence that an effective system of conscription could be introduced. In peacetime, therefore, we must make the all-volunteer force work rather than embroil ourselves in a debilitating controversy about the draft.

Granting that conscription is not in the offing, could management steps be taken to improve the utilization of manpower within the framework of the all-volunteer force? Almost all the proposals for doing so that have been made share one difficulty: they fail to address the core issue of how to get qualified young men into the combat arms and aboard warships without using direct compulsion. Neither lowering the physical or mental standards for men, nor increasing the number of women, nor relying more heavily on civilian personnel or older members of the military suits the imperatives of the combat arms. What is needed is a way of attracting a more representative cross section of young men to the combat arms and related tasks. Or, to put it differently, we need to find a way of obtaining the analogue of the peacetime draftee in the all-volunteer context.

I believe there is a way to do that. But it requires us to overhaul the definition of military service as well as the machinery of recruitment in the all-volunteer force. We must recognize that those who enter the military for a short hiatus in their lives have different motivations from those who might make a longer commitment; and, recognizing that difference, the army can set up a two-track personnel system that distinguishes between a citizen soldier and a career soldier.[16]

To have a workable conscription requires a national consensus, especially within the relevant youth population, as to the need for conscription. Such a consensus does not exist currently and seems unlikely in the foreseeable future.

89

An initial step would be to introduce post-service educational benefits modeled after the GI Bill of World War II and limit them to a new citizen-soldier track. The other features of that track would be short enlistments, lower active-duty pay, and assignment to the combat arms and other labor-intensive tasks. The rationale is that a GI Bill would not be truly cost effective unless it was connected with a lower-paid short-enlistment option (not any longer than two years, the term served by the old draftee).

Linking GI Bill eligibility to a short-term enlistment would maximize the likelihood of attracting those youths for whom high recruit pay and enlistment bonuses are not inducements; and the low-pay no-bonus feature would minimize the siphoning off of those already inclined to join the military. With no presumption that civilian skills would be acquired in the military, the terms of such service would be honest and unambiguous, thus alleviating a major source of post-entry discontent in the all-volunteer force.

Although it must be acknowledged that the actual outcomes of any military personnel policy cannot be foreseen with exactitude, such a citizen-soldier track, with its educational benefits, would probably be more attractive to black youths than to white youths. Among male youths coming from poor families, a higher percentage of blacks than whites are likely to attend college.[17] Probably, too, the percentage of black entrants who selected the citizen-soldier track would be less than the percentage joining in the late 1970s—between 30 and 35 percent—but close to the figure for the early 1980s—around 25 percent. Almost certainly, the number of blacks entering the army would be greater if a citizen-soldier option were available than if the draft were reintroduced.

*B*ecause the black reenlistment rate will almost surely continue to exceed the rate for whites, the percentage of blacks in the career force of the military will continue to increase--whether we adopt a new recruitment system, maintain the present system, or go back to a draft.

If a citizen-soldier track were properly monitored, it could open another avenue for black recruitment into the officer corps. It could do this by encouraging black college graduates with prior-enlistment service—GI Bill recipients—to enter officer commissioning programs.

The career soldier, in contrast, would initially enlist for a minimum of four years. He or she would receive entitlements and compensation similar to those in the current system, but with significant increases in payment at the time of the first reenlistment and throughout the senior NCO grades. In certain skill areas with extreme shortages, special reenlistment bonuses (and even, perhaps, off-scale pay) would be required.

Many career members would be trained in technical skills, though others would make up the future cadre in a variety of military specialties. Present contributory educational assistance programs would be continued. Ideally, strong consideration would be given to allowing career NCOs to take sabbaticals, during which they would study engineering or science for future technical work in the military. Steps such as these would go a long way toward retaining the experienced and trained personnel required for a complex and technical military force.

The two-track system outlined here has advantages beyond immediate considerations of manpower. It would begin to resolve the issue of the benefits and burdens of military service. Broadly speaking, the burdens—service at low pay in combat units and in tasks with low civilian transferability—would become much more the responsibility of the middle class than they are at present in the market-driven all-volunteer force. The benefits—career progression, technical training, and decent compensation—would still be most attractive to youths with limited opportunities in civilian life, a group that, for an indeterminate future, will still be disproportionately black. Moreover, because the black reenlistment rate will almost surely continue to exceed the rate for whites, the percentage of blacks in the career force of the military will continue to increase--whether we adopt a new recruitment system, maintain the present system, or go back to a draft.

To support policies that accentuate the tracking of lower-class and minority youths into the enlisted ranks is devious; and to rationalize the outcome by calling it the result of voluntary and desirable workings of the economic marketplace is perverse.

Conclusion

Issues of recruitment and retention in the military are necessarily embedded in a larger social context. In considering those issues, we do not want to be so overwhelmed with data, so bedeviled with rival sets of numbers, that we hardly understand, much less address, the key considerations.

It is a social reality that the enlisted ranks of the armed forces will never draw proportionately from middle- and upper-class youths. But to support policies that accentuate the tracking of lower-class and minority youths into the enlisted ranks is devious; and to rationalize the outcome by calling it the result of voluntary and desirable workings of the economic marketplace is perverse. The boot of unemployment more than the unseen hand of Adam Smith has accounted for the change in the recruitment picture of the early 1980s. This is not to argue that the composition of the enlisted ranks ought to be perfectly calibrated with the composition of the larger society, but it is to ask what kind of society grounds military service on marketplace principles and thereby excuses its privileged from serving in the ranks of its army.

Endnotes

1. Franklin A. Thomas, *Youth Unemployment and National Service* (New York: Ford Foundation, April 1983), p. 8.

2. Gates Commission, *The Report of the President's Commission on an All-Volunteer Armed Force* (Washington, D.C.: GPO, 1970). For a critique of the Gates Commission's assumptions, see Charles C. Moskos and John H. Faris, "Beyond the Marketplace," in Andrew J. Goodpaster, Lloyd H. Elliott, and J. Allan Hovey, Jr., eds., *Toward a Consensus on Military Service* (New York: Pergamon, 1982), pp. 131-151.

3. The best overview of blacks in the military is Martin Binkin and Mark J. Eitelberg with Alvin J. Schexnider and M. Martin Smith, *Blacks and the Military* (Washington, D.C.: The Brookings Institution, 1982). The classic study on institutional racism in the armed forces is John S. Butler, "Inequality in the Military," *American Sociological Review* 41 (October 1976): 807-818. See also John S. Butler and Kenneth L. Wilson, "The American Soldier Revisited: Race Relations and the Military," *Social Science Quarterly* 59:3 (December 1978): 451-467; and John S. Butler and Malcolm D. Holmes, "Perceived Discrimination and the Military Experience,"

Journal of Political and Military Sociology 9 (Spring 1981): 17-30. On the issue of black consciousness in the military, see Alvin J. Schexnider, "The Development of Racial Solidarity in the Armed Forces," *Journal of Black Studies* 5:4 (June 1975): 415-435; and Alvin J. Schexnider, "Expectations from the Ranks," *American Behavioral Scientist* 19:5 (May/June 1976): 523-541. A perceptive account of the military's effort to cope with racial strife and of the formation of the Defense Race Relations Institute is Richard O. Hope, *Racial Strife in the U.S. Military* (New York: Praeger, 1979).

4. *Blacks and the Military,* p. 66.

5. Harley L. S. Browning, Sally C. Lopreato, and Dudley L. Poston, Jr., "Income and Veterans' Status," *American Sociological Review* 38 (1973): 74-85; and Sally C. Lopreato and Dudley L. Poston, Jr., "Differences in Earnings and Earning Ability Between Black Veterans and Nonveterans in the United States," *Social Science Quarterly* 57 (1977): 750-766.

6. Bernard Beck, "The Military as a Welfare Institution," in Charles C. Moskos, ed., *Public Opinion and the Military Establishment* (Beverly Hills: Sage, 1971), pp. 137-148.

7. Richard V. L. Cooper, *Military Manpower and the All-Volunteer Force* (Santa Monica, Calif.: Rand, 1977), p. 139; and David J. Armor, *Mental Ability and Army Job Performance* (Santa Monica, Calif.: Rand, 1981).

8. Higher mental test scores do, however, appear to characterize those who successfully complete highly technical courses of military instruction, in contrast to those who do not (Armor, *Mental Ability*). As a caveat to studies relating individual test scores to military performance measures, I would warn the reader that such research is typically based on relations between an individual's traits and his or her performance, thereby remaining innocent of social-psychological factors. In the military environment, however, tasks are almost always performed in groups, and the dynamics of these groups can enhance or degrade individual performance. We would all be better informed if studies of military performance placed performance in group contexts.

9. For the World War II data, see Samuel A. Stouffer et al., *The American Soldier: Combat and Its Aftermath* (Princeton: Princeton University Press, 1949), pp. 36-41. On the Korean War, see Roger L. Egbert et al., *Fighter 1: An Analysis of Combat Fighters and Non-Fighters* (Washington, D.C.: HumRRO, 1957). A good summary of the literature dealing with quality and performance in the military is Juri Toomepuu, *Soldier Capability—Army Combat Effectiveness—SCACE* (Fort Harrison, Ind.: U.S. Army Soldier Support Center, February 1981). A survey of Army officers reported that dissatisfaction with soldier quality became stronger with decreasing rank and increasing proximity to troops; *U.S. Army War College Study on Officer Professionalism* (Carlisle Barracks, Pa.: U.S. Army War College, 1979), p. 12.

10. David R. Segal, Barbara Ann Lynch, and John D. Blair, "The Changing American Soldier: Work-Related Attitudes of U.S. Army Personnel in World War II and the 1970s," *American Journal of Sociology* 85 (1979): 95-108.

11. Unpublished data run made for Choongsoo Kim et al., *The All Volunteer Force: An Analysis of Youth Participation, Attrition, and Reenlistment* (Columbus: Ohio State University, Center for Human Resource Research, 1980).

12. Stephen D. Wesbrook, "Sociopolitical Aliena-tion and Military Efficiency," *Armed Forces and Society* 6 (1980): 170-189.

13. Gilbert Badillo and G. David Curry, "The Social Incidence of Vietnam Casualties: Social Class or Race," *Armed Forces and Society* 2 (1976): 397-406.

14. Richard W. Hunter and Gary R. Nelson, "Eight Years with the All-Volunteer Armed Forces," in Brent Scowcroft, ed., *Military Service in the United States* (Englewood Cliffs, N.J.: Prentice-Hall, 1982), pp. 102-104.

15. Binkin et al., *Blacks and the Military,* p. 66.

16. A more detailed discussion of this proposal is given in Charles C. Moskos, "Making the All-

Volunteer Force Work: A National Service
Approach," *Foreign Affairs* 60 (Fall 1981): 17-34.

17. U.S. Bureau of the Census, *Current Population Reports,* "School Enrollment—Social and
Economic Characteristics of Students," series P-20,
no. 362, issued May 1981. It is also true that blacks
in the military have higher educational expectations
than whites (Binkin et al., *Blacks and the Military,*
p. 50).

8. CHOICE, JUSTICE, AND REPRESENTATION

Robert K. Fullinwider

R acial imbalance in the armed forces has been a source of continuing concern and controversy during the past two decades. The questions of whether racial imbalance is in fact a problem and, if so, what kind of problem it is and what can be done about it are questions that elicit little agreement. In this essay, I want to sort out some of the issues and hold up to light some of the implications of alternative policy choices.[1]

Reasons for Concern

Since 1970, the percentage of blacks in the U.S. military has doubled. The army's enlisted ranks are about 30 percent black; the marine corps, about 20 percent. This growing racial disproportion (blacks make up about 13 percent of the youth population) is fueled by both volunteer and reenlistment rates that are higher for blacks than for whites.

Is this imbalance in the army (and to a lesser extent the marine corps) something to worry about? Is it undesirable? Some people think it is. The reasons they give for being worried can be categorized under two headings: prudential and moral. The prudential reasons have to do with the possible ill effects of the imbalance on the army itself, on the black community, and on the country as a whole. The moral reasons are rooted in ideas of fairness and democratic representation.

The reasons [some people] give for being worried [about the racial balance of the armed forces] can be categorized under two headings: prudential and moral.

Prudential Concerns

The first prudential concern is that the growth of black enlistments could harm the army. This would occur if black enlistments—

- produced a tipping effect, causing white enlistments to drop precipitously;

- fueled bad race relations within units; or

- undermined the political reliability of the combat arms.[2]

The second prudential concern is that the large overrepresentation of blacks in the army might be bad for the black community itself. The influx of black youths into the services might strip the black community of an important human resource, impoverishing it even more.[3] Further, it has been argued that if the army came to be seen by the larger society as a haven for minorities, the service could lose its viability as a means of upward mobility for black youths.[4]

The third prudential concern is that the growing racial imbalance in the army could undermine the institutional legitimacy of the military, as citizens ceased to identify with and support an increasingly unrepresentative, "alien" armed force.[5] This result would be bad not only for the military, but also for the country. Moreover, there are fears about what could happen in the event of a war, when initial casualties would be 30 percent or more black. This might prove politically indigestible. Public reaction could divide the nation, especially along lines of color. The shocking and graphically depicted deaths of a disproportionately large number of black youths might traumatize the black community, prompting it—or significant portions of it—into active resistance to the government's war policy. This response, too, would be undesirable for the country as a whole, aside from severely threatening the gains the black community had made in becoming integrated into the larger society.[6]

The shocking and graphically depicted deaths of a disproportionately large number of black youths might traumatize the black community, prompting it—or significant portions of it—into active resistance to the government's war policy.

At present, however, a tipping effect is not taking place in the army; race relations there appear to be at least as good as, if not better than, they are in society at large; and neither our allies nor our enemies appear to be changing their military strategies in response to the number of blacks in the U.S. Army. Moreover, in recent years civilian support for military institutions has been increasing rather than decreasing. Finally, the nation is not at war, so no blacks are dying in combat.

Thus, the threat posed by racial imbalance lies in *possibilities*—the possibility that tipping will occur in the future, that race relations will deteriorate, or, in the event of war, that high black casualties will deplete the best of black youth or spark resistance in the black community. Were some of the more extreme scenarios to be realized, considerable and serious harm to the military, the black community, and the country could occur.

> *Policies that block or impede black entry into the armed forces must be predicated on more than risk aversion.*

But the likelihood that the worst outcomes will materialize is not terribly high, although different informed observers will undoubtedly disagree in the subjective probabilities they assign to the various possibilities. Although conceivably the country could be torn apart and the black community thrown into open rebellion if a war produced 30-40 percent black casualties, less traumatic forms of distress seem more likely.

In situations where we face a small likelihood of a grave harm, we face a most difficult kind of choice. Were nothing else at stake, we could simply adopt a strongly risk-averse policy. We could say that if racial imbalance created any risk at all of a very unlikely, but very undesirable, state of affairs, we would take whatever actions were necessary to restore balance. But risk-averse policies in this case come with a price tag. To diminish the inflow of blacks into the army to proportionate levels would mean depriving many young blacks of an opportunity they evidently value highly, if we may take their current behavior as evidence. Given this quite real cost, policies that block or impede black entry into the armed forces must be predicated on more than risk aversion.

Moreover, in evaluating prudential concerns about the racial make-up of the enlisted ranks of the army, we must take account of the possibility that

As a nation we may be overreacting to a danger more imaginary than real, and white policy-makers may be disposed to magnify the seriousness of problems arising from black overrepresentation.

whites may be too easily alarmed by black overrepresentation. As a nation we may be overreacting to a danger more imaginary than real, and white policy-makers may be disposed to magnify the seriousness of problems arising from black overrepresentation. Consequently, it seems reasonable to set a high threshold of proof, requiring that evidence of the threat from racial imbalance be ample and strongly persuasive, if not compelling. Scenarios with merely some degree of plausibility are insufficient bases for policies that deny opportunities to blacks.

Of all the prudential concerns discussed, the worry about high black casualties and their impact on the black community and the nation seems most troubling. We need not fear a convulsive reaction in the black community to feel moved to avoid potentially high black casualties. We might simply view the collective impact of concentrated casualties as being directly injurious to the black community and, just as we might want to take steps to see that extensive casualties are not concentrated in a single geographical community, we might want to take comparable steps to see that extensive casualties are not concentrated in a single cultural, racial, or ethnic community.

We could reduce the potential for disproportionately high black casualty rates in any of several ways—by manipulating enlistment incentives, by channeling blacks into units or specialties that generally experience low casualty rates, by imposing quotas on the number of blacks permitted to enlist, or by reinstituting a draft.

For example, one suggestion for reducing the number of blacks exposed to danger envisages a special two-year tour of duty for the combat arms, at low pay with delayed benefits in the form of substantial aid for a college education. The idea is that this incentive package would attract just enough middle-class, college-bound white youths to reduce black representation in the combat arms.[7] Whether such a change would in fact bring about a reduction in black representation is debatable. The second possibility— outright use of race to make assignments within the military—would probably undermine morale severely and damage race relations within the military. Imposing quotas on black enlistments and using a draft to fill the ranks might reduce the percentage of blacks in the army and, thus, their percentage in the combat arms, but it would withhold the opportunity to serve from some blacks who would otherwise be qualified.

Moral Concerns

The group that worries about racial imbalance for moral reasons would find the present situation in the army objectionable even if it could be known that none of the ill effects just listed would come about. The direct moral objections take two paths. The first focuses on the *process* by which the imbalance is generated. It views the present policy of relying solely upon volunteers to staff the military as exploiting the economic weakness of blacks. The second line of objection focuses on the *fact* of white middle-class underrepresentation: democracy requires a representative military as a matter of principle.[8]

Process: The Issue of Exploitation

The view that the all-volunteer policy is unjustly exploitative has been expressed by one congressional critic as follows:

> The fatal defect in the All-Volunteer Force is that . . . it is not a volunteer system at all. The AVF has proven an unjust and inequitable system of economic and racial conscription. A system in which those who have the least in our society are offered the opportunity to be trained to risk all in exchange for the very thing they have been denied by the society they are asked to defend, a job.[9]

To such critics, the all-volunteer force is conscription through poverty.[10]

We understand in a general way what these complaints point to. They picture a situation in which a young black faces joblessness and poverty unless he elects military service. He is therefore forced by circumstances to enlist; he has no choice. Military policy takes advantage of the economic desperation

To [some] critics, the all-volunteer force is conscription through poverty. They picture a situation in which a young black faces joblessness and poverty unless he elects military service.

of the youth to enlist him, and the policy is therefore exploitative and unjust.

How shall we assess these charges? First, having no choice is not incompatible with acting voluntarily. In *The Nichomachean Ethics,* Aristotle describes a situation in which a sea captain jettisons his cargo in a storm to keep his ship afloat.[11] We can say the captain was forced by circumstances, that he had no choice but, even so, that he acted voluntarily. But when we say the captain had no choice, we are not speaking strictly. He had two options: dumping his cargo or not dumping it. What we mean is that one of the options (saving the ship by throwing off the cargo) is so much better than the other (sinking with the cargo on board) that no reasonable person would choose any differently.

Likewise, the young black who faces unemployment has the option, strictly speaking, of enduring that condition rather than enlisting. His situation is not one in which there is literally only one choice, but one in which there is only one choice worth making. We should put aside as hyperbole the claim that the all-volunteer force is not really voluntary but is really a form of conscription.

S uppose, for example, that the black youth had to choose between unemployment and a full scholarship to an excellent university. Can we imagine any- one's condemning the university's offer as conscription through poverty? Do we doubt here that the youth's choice is voluntary?

Doing so does not, however, dispose of the charges of exploitation and injustice, because it should be apparent by now that what underlies the complaint against the all-volunteer force is not so much the *structure* of choices facing black youths, but their *content.* Suppose, for example, that the black youth had to choose between unemployment and a full scholarship to an excellent university. Can we imagine anyone's condemning the university's offer as conscription through poverty? Do we doubt here that the youth's choice is voluntary? It is important to the critic's charge, then, that the choice faced by the youth is between unemployment and military service—and it is likewise important that military service be an undesirable option.

We would not do an injustice to a black youth by offering as an option to unemployment something that was desirable for its own sake, such as the scholarship. The hidden premise in the critic's argument, therefore, is that military service is a bad

102

choice to have. In fact, given the vehemence of the objection to the all-volunteer system, the underlying premise must be that military service is something no one would do willingly. The black recruit serves because of his desperation. The military is the lesser evil among his options, but an evil it remains. If we considered military service to be a positive good, like the scholarship, why would we be distressed that the youth had this alternative to unemployment?

Once we make this hidden premise plain, it becomes clear, I think, that one cannot plausibly hold the position that the all-volunteer policy is inherently unjust and exploitative. Suppose, for instance, we offered enlistees a starting salary of $25,000 a year. In that case, as in the scholarship case, we would consider the black youth fortunate to have such an opportunity. It would be difficult, indeed, to retain the idea that the all-volunteer policy was exploiting him.

Given the vehemence of the objection to the all-volunteer system, the underlying premise must be that military service is something no one would do willingly. The black recruit serves because of his desperation.

Exploitation, at least as we commonly think of it, occurs when someone takes advantage of someone else's weakness to get something from him for less than he otherwise would have been *willing* to accept. If we took advantage of the limited options facing the black youth by offering him a place in the military at a wage of, say, 60 percent of the average wage for unskilled, entry-level civilian jobs, then our action would seem exploitative. But offering the youth military service at $25,000 would not seem exploitative because we assume he would see the opportunity as a very desirable one and would choose it in any case.

Or we might view exploitation as taking advantage of someone's weakness to get something from him for less than we *ought* to pay him. Even in this sense, most of us would not consider the black youth who received a starting salary of $25,000 to be exploited, because we would be likely to consider that salary as at least equal to what we ought to pay someone for undergoing the rigors and risks of military service.

If, then, the all-volunteer system is not inherently exploitative, the complaint of the critics really becomes a complaint about the compensation provided by the all-volunteer force. The real charge must be that military service provides too little reward to be more than an experience that must be endured for the sake of escaping poverty. If the level of compensation were above some threshold of adequacy, the charge of exploitation would have to be withdrawn. Is this entire debate, then, over pay scales, over the level of compensation?

If the level of compensation were above some threshold of adequacy, the charge of exploitation would have to be withdrawn. Is this entire debate, then, over pay scales, over the level of compensation?

Those who are profoundly distressed at what they take to be the injustice of the all-volunteer policy certainly believe their complaint goes far deeper than a quarrel about starting pay. They talk of the unfairness of blacks' bearing a disproportionate share of the defense burden.[12] But if military service is fully compensated and if the people in the military want to be there, then it is not a burden. They speak of blacks' being *forced* to carry a disproportionate part of the defense load.[13] But no one is literally forced to serve, and if the all-volunteer force offered very attractive compensation, as, for example, in the $25,000 example, we would not be able to say that anyone was forced to serve, even in the most extended, exaggerated sense of the word. The matter, therefore, does appear to come down to a question of the level of compensation after all.

Since its inception in 1973 (with the exception of the period FY 1977-80), the all-volunteer force has offered a starting compensation package roughly equivalent or superior to average civilian entry-level wages for unskilled youths.* The critic, in order to sustain his charge of exploitation, must believe that the unemployed black youth would view military life as distinctly less desirable than comparable civilian alternatives.

The objection might be made that my assessment of the critics' argument misses the point. I treat the military as if it were a peacetime institution when in fact it exists to fight wars. In war, soldiers are exposed to death and injury on an extensive scale. In

---

*In 1987, Basic Military Compensation for a first-term enlistee (E-1) with no dependents was around $12,000 a year. By contrast, a full-time civilian job at the minimum wage would pay around $7,000 (Department of Defense, "Selected Military Compensation Tables, January 1987 Pay Rates" [Office of the Assistant Secretary of Defense, Directorate of Compensation]).

joining the military, blacks are being asked to put their lives on the line as a condition for economic advancement. It is inappropriate to view military and civilian occupations as equivalent alternatives. This was the complaint of the congressional critic referred to earlier.

It is true that a military force may go to war; soldiers may be called on to fight and die. But it is also true that the military is a peacetime institution and is generally not at war. The all-volunteer system was conceived from the beginning as a peacetime operation. Any major military engagement would call for a resumption of the draft. A young person—black or white—who considers military service today must weigh the benefits he will gain against the drawbacks of service, one of which is the risk of being injured or killed in war. This risk is composed of the risk that war will occur, the risk of being exposed to combat should war occur, and the risk of suffering injury or death should one be exposed to combat. Of course, wars can differ in their scope, lethality, and duration, and different kinds of wars also differ in their likelihood of occurring. In any case, a peacetime recruit must count the overall risks to him as not terribly high, unless it is a time when war is clearly imminent.* He will find military service an attractive option if the combination of its economic and non-economic returns compensates fully not only for the unpleasantnesses of service but also for the risks. Thus, the issue seems to come back again to a question of the proper level of compensation.

The heart of the critic's concern might be expressed this way: it is wrong that the black youth must choose between unemployment and the risk of death, however small. Because of his desperate circumstances, he will be tempted to assign a lower value to and accept less compensation for the risk

> *The heart of the critic's concern might be expressed this way: it is wrong that the black youth must choose between unemployment and the risk of death.*

*During the Vietnam War only 6 percent of the active duty troops were committed to combat. Overall, the risk of combat service was so low for Vietnam-era servicemen that life insurance companies did not charge extra premiums for military personnel, except for pilots and others on unusually hazardous missions (Lawrence M. Baskir and William A. Strauss, *Chance and Circumstance* [New York: Vintage Books, 1978], p. 52).

than (in our judgment) he should. In contrast, the white middle-class youth, having other options besides unemployment and military service, will set a value on the risk of death more in line with what we think appropriate.[14] If this is our concern, we can see that the problem would be alleviated if the all-volunteer force increased its compensation package to a level that would attract middle-class whites. We could then be confident that the recruitment system did not exploit the presumed willingness of blacks to undervalue their lives.

Many who object that the all-volunteer system is exploitative propose a draft as a solution. But enough has been said, I think, to show the incongruity of reducing exploitation with a draft. Because a draft would allow compulsion to be used in securing manpower, it would put a damper on the economic compensation offered by the military; reduced wage rates would be offered. If, as the critics suppose, black youths are facing the choice between unemployment and service, then many of them would volunteer anyway, even under the reduced wage. At that point, however, we would be getting their voluntary service at a level of compensation below what would attract middle-class whites and, therefore, below the level we think appropriate for risking death and injury. Thus, we would truly be taking advantage of the willingness of these blacks to undervalue their lives. Moreover, some blacks who would not volunteer at that lower level of compensation would be drafted and would thus be forced to serve at a wage they would already have rejected as unacceptable. This would be exploitation, too. Finally, there would be some blacks who, having only the options of unemployment and service, would neither volunteer at the new reduced compensation nor get drafted; they would be left in unemployment.

If, as the critics suppose, black youths are facing the choice between unemployment and service, then many of them would volunteer anyway, even under the reduced wage.

It is hard, then, to see how any of these blacks would have received justice—the ones who would serve anyway at reduced compensation, the ones who would be compelled to serve, or the ones who would be left mired in unemployment. Considered simply from the point of view of justice for desperate blacks, a draft would introduce legal compulsion, diminish valued opportunities, and increase exploitation.

Fact: The Issue of Principle

Independently of whether the racial imbalance in the military is a sign of exploitation, it has been taken by some as an affront to the principles of democracy. James Fallows, for example, has argued that the racial imbalance "has destructive spiritual effects in a nation based on the democratic creed. . . . The military has been an avenue of opportunity for many young blacks and they may well be first-class fighting men, but they do not represent the nation."[15]

In what sense does democracy require a representative military? In what way does the current military fail to represent America?

To represent something is to stand for it. Clearly, I think, we want the military to stand for us in the sense that we want it peopled by soldiers and sailors who understand and value the ends that the military must serve. In this moral sense, our military represents us when its members share and endorse the same basic commitments and values reflected in the population at large. An alien force would be composed of individuals who are prepared to fight for pay but who do not understand, value, or subscribe to the goals and aspirations of the culture they protected and the political institutions they defended.

If the racial imbalance in the military signifies a failure of representation in this moral sense, it must be because the black recruits are alien. We would have to hold that they are so alienated from American society that they undertake service exclusively as an economic choice and that they possess little commitment to American institutions and values. In contrast, if we viewed the current military as composed of American youths with American values, what further moral, as oppposed to prudential, interest could we have in representativeness? Why would we have to be morally concerned that the military mirror social, ethnic, racial, or other demographic patterns found in society as a whole?

Under a system of compulsory selection, of course, we would be concerned about demographic representativeness because that would be a sign of fairness in the selection procedure. At least, we would be concerned about it if we thought that,

Considered simply from the point of view of justice for desperate blacks, a draft would introduce legal compulsion, diminish valued opportunities, and increase exploitation.

among those liable to induction, selection should be more or less random. Random selection recommends itself when we must distribute to some, but not all, an unwanted burden and when no one especially deserves the burden or has a special claim to avoid it. Under a system of self-selection, however, in which outcomes reflect the distribution of desire, there is no *a priori* reason to expect the outcomes to match what would have been achieved in a random selection.

Quite obviously many young persons, black and white, enlist in the military for economic reasons. But this does not preclude their viewing the military at the same time as an honorable form of service, a way to contribute to the common good and to peace.

I do not think that Fallows and other critics have borne the burden of showing that black American youths are less patriotic and less loyal than white youths, or poor youths less patriotic and loyal than middle-class youths. Yet unless this is the case, I do not see a basis for claiming any failure of moral representativeness in the military, even if we recognize a failure of demographic representativeness. Quite obviously many young persons, black and white, enlist in the military for economic reasons. But this does not preclude their viewing the military at the same time as an honorable form of service, a way to contribute to the common good and to peace. In fact, the very thing that may attract a youth to service is that it is a decent economic opportunity that also allows him to serve larger and worthier ends than his own material advancement. We believe that white middle-class youths are capable of this kind of complex motivation (commissioned officers, after all, do not serve in the military for peanuts). Do we believe that poor and black youths are less capable of it?

Endnotes

1. This essay is based on my chapter "The All-Volunteer Force and Racial Balance," in Robert K. Fullinwider, ed., *Morality and Military Service: Essays on the All-Volunteer Force and Its Alternatives* (Totawa, N.J.: Rowman and Allanheld, 1983).

2. See Morris Janowitz, "Focus on Blacks in Military," *Focus* 3 (June 1975): 3.

3. Martin Binkin estimates that 42 percent of black males born between 1957 and 1962 who would probably have been eligible for service had enlisted in

the military by 1981. See Martin Binkin and Mark J. Eitelberg with Alvin J. Schexnider and M. Martin Smith, *Blacks and the Military* (Washington, D.C.: The Brookings Institution, 1982), pp. 66, 98.

4. See Charles C. Moskos, "Making the All-Volunteer Force Work: A National Service Approach," *Foreign Affairs* 60 (Fall 1981): 20.

5. Ibid.

6. See Charles C. Moskos, "Symposium: Race in the United States Military," *Armed Forces and Society,* 6 (Summer 1981): 589f.

7. Moskos, "Making the All-Volunteer Force Work," pp. 24-26.

8. See Janowitz, op. cit.

9. Congressman John Cavanaugh, *Synergist* (Winter 1980), p. 14, reprinted in *Presidential Commission on National Service and National Commission on Voluntarism,* hearing before the Subcommittee on Child and Human Development, Committee on Labor and Human Resources, U.S. Senate, 96th Congress, 2nd Session, 13 March 1980, p. 432.

10. Joseph Califano, "Playing the Draft Card," *The Washington Post,* January 27, 1980, B7; Roger Landrum and Harris Wofford, remarks in *National Youth Service: What's at Stake. Report of a Conference Sponsored by the Committee for the Study of National Service* (Washington, D.C.: Potomac Institute, 1980), pp. 4, 14.

11. *Nichomachean Ethics,* book III, 1110a-10b2.

12. See the assertion by Congressman Lucien Nedzi in *Hearings on Military Posture and H.R. 1872,* Committee on Armed Services, House of Representatives, 96th Congress, 1st Session, February-April 1979, part 5, p. 182.

13. General William Westmoreland, interview in *U.S. News and World Report*, May 17, 1980.

14. The idea of placing an appropriate value on risk of death needs some comment. As used in the text, the phrase "value on the risk of death" suggests some objective appraisal of value. Otherwise, any value an individual put on the risk of death which

realistically reflected his own circumstances, options, and desires would be appropriate. If there is some objective basis for saying that a person is really undervaluing his life, we need to know about it. I imagine that we would try to spell out the basis like this: the risks a person takes should reflect his overall value system (e.g., what the person views as the purposes of his life, what moral worth he assigns to the ends for which he risks his life, and so on). But when a person is desperate, the risks he takes will be as likely to reflect his condition as to reflect his considered assessment of the meaning and value of his life. So the standard of appropriate risk taking ought to be a hypothetical situation in which there were ample choices.

When a middle-class white youth assumes the risks of service, he meets this standard because his actual condition matches the hypothetical condition; when an unemployed black youth assumes the risks, he does not meet the standard because his actual circumstances fail to reflect the hypothetical condition.

These comments are admittedly vague. The notion of the objective basis requires further development, and I do not know whether it can be done successfully. But the complaints I am considering do, I believe, reflect a gut intuition of such a notion, and the text explores the implications of that intuition.

15. James Fallows, "The Draft: Why the Country Needs It," *Atlantic* 245 (April 1980), reprinted in Jason Berger, ed., *The Military Draft,* The Reference Shelf, vol. 53, no. 4 (New York: H. W. Wilson Company, 1981), 79. See also James Fallows, *National Defense* (New York: Random House, 1981), pp. 123-138.

9. PUBLIC ATTITUDES

A. Wade Smith

The personnel policies of the military are and always have been subject to influence from public opinion. Changes in public opinion have led to changes both in the requirements we place on our military forces and in the extent to which we subscribe to the belief that military service is an obligation of citizenship.[1]

Nowhere is the influence of public opinion more important than in matters regarding blacks and women in uniform. For most of this nation's history, blacks served in segregated units (when they were allowed to serve at all), and women served primarily as nurses and in rear-echelon administrative jobs.

President Truman's Executive Order 9981, issued in 1948, began a process that led to the elimination of racial segregation in the military. All-female units, such as the Women's Army Corps, were eliminated as a result of reforms begun in the 1970s. The nation's political leaders instituted those changes either in anticipation of the public's accepting the change or in response to public pressure.

The current composition of the military is the result of public opposition to the draft, an opposition that was heightened by the nation's prolonged and costly involvement in Vietnam. In response to public opinion, President Nixon allowed conscription to lapse in 1972; since 1973, the nation has been defended by an all-volunteer force.

The all-volunteer force made it possible for middle-class youths, who had provided some of the most vocal opposition to the draft and to the Vietnam conflict, to avoid military service. One result has

The current composition of the military is the result of public opposition to the draft, an opposition that was heightened by the nation's prolonged and costly involvement in Vietnam.

been that the ranks of the armed forces have come increasingly to be filled by the poor and by blacks. The all-volunteer force also has a much higher percentage of women than did the draft-era military, and women have been assigned to a number of duties from which they were once excluded.

Now that these consequences of an all-volunteer force are fully apparent, it is appropriate to ask whether or not the public approves. To answer that question, this research uses the General Social Survey (GSS) conducted by the National Opinion Research Center in February 1982. The results reported here come from interviews with 1,570 respondents (1,323 whites and 247 blacks)—a national sample sufficient to represent the American public to an accuracy of within 4 percent. All the interviews were administered by professionals who contacted the respondents in their homes and interviewed them in person. All the blacks were interviewed by black interviewers, and more than 90 percent of the whites were interviewed by white interviewers. The survey was financed by the National Science Foundation and the Ford Foundation.

The 1982 GSS is particularly valuable for three reasons. First, it is the first survey to inquire into the opinions of the public concerning the representation of blacks and women in the armed forces. Until the survey was conducted, commentaries about the all-volunteer force, especially suggestions that its changing composition would affect public confidence in the military, had been based on speculation. The survey allows us to assess whether the speculation has been close to the mark or has simply reflected the personal predispositions of the commentators.

Second, the 1982 GSS took extra steps to obtain interviews from a specially designed subsample of blacks. As a result, the subsample of black cases is somewhat larger and more representative than the number of black cases in typical national samples: 247 rather than the usual 150-180. The larger size allows us to disaggregate the black subsample and examine differences in opinion among blacks.

Now that these consequences of an all-volunteer force are fully apparent, it is appropriate to ask whether or not the public approves.

Third, the respondents were asked questions about a number of topics, not just about the military. This allows us, among other things, to determine whether attitudes toward certain military issues are correlated with the presence or absence of racial prejudice. We can speculate that prejudiced and nonprejudiced people will disagree over whether or not there are too many blacks in the military. We cannot, however, discover whether people are prejudiced by asking them directly. Instead, we draw an inference by asking them how they feel about other issues—school desegregation, for example. If some white respondents say they would be uncomfortable having their children attend a school with even a few black students, we can infer that they are highly prejudiced. By posing a series of such questions, we can place respondents on a scale ranging from "very prejudiced" to "not prejudiced at all."

Sometimes public opinion tends to cluster across an array of issues (such clustering would allow us to say that people have a structure of beliefs). In this study, we will seek not only to determine whether certain kinds of people have similar opinions on particular issues, but also to assess the magnitude of this type of clustering. For example, we may find that a large percentage of the population believes there are too many blacks in the armed services, and we may also find that a large percentage of the population has low confidence in the military. The question we will attempt to answer is whether these are essentially the same people.

It is particularly important that we examine the clustering of views about the composition of the military and views about confidence in the military, because one of the chief complaints made by critics of the all-volunteer force is that the changing racial and sexual composition of the services could undermine public confidence in, and support for, the nation's defense establishment. Thus, our examination of clustering could help settle some long-standing arguments about the all-volunteer force and, by extension, about the national service program that some people have proposed as a replacement for it.

One of the chief complaints made by critics of the all-volunteer force is that the changing racial and sexual composition of the services could undermine public confidence in, and support for, the nation's defense establishment.

Attitudes Toward the Racial Composition of the Military

The responses to two questions in the GSS give us our basic data on opinions about black overrepresentation in the military. Each question was posed to a randomly chosen half of the survey respondents. The first question mentioned the percentage of all military personnel who are black; the other mentioned the percentage for the army alone.

The questions were:

At the present time, about 22 percent of the armed forces [33 percent of the army] are black. All things considered, do you think there are too many blacks in the armed forces [army], about the right number, or should there be more blacks in the armed forces [army]?

As table 9-1 shows, approximately the same percentage of respondents answered "too many blacks" to the question about the army alone as to the question about the services as a whole.* The breakdowns for the "about right" and "too few" categories are also very similar from one question to the other. In fact, statistically there is no difference between the overall responses to the two questions. We can therefore combine the two groups of respondents, doubling the number of respondents designated as the overall survey population and producing a somewhat more representative sample of the general population.

*M*ore people believed there were too few blacks in the military than believed there were too many, a finding at odds with the general tenor of the remarks made by many critics of the all-volunteer force.

Perhaps the most notable figure is the small number of people—only 12.5 percent—who said they thought there were too many blacks in the military. In fact, more people believed there were too few blacks in the military than believed there were too many, a finding at odds with the general tenor of the remarks made by many critics of the all-volunteer force. It may well be that some commentators have overestimated the level of public concern about this issue. A closer look at the people who make up the small percentage that find blacks in the military to be too numerous is clearly in order, since the identity of

---

*In the tables in this chapter, columns may not add up to 100 percent, because of rounding or other statistical operations.

Table 9-1

Public Opinion About the Percentage of Blacks in the Army and in the Armed Forces as a Whole

	Army	Armed Forces	Combined Results
Too many blacks[a]	12.8%	12.1%	12.5%
(Number)	(89)	(82)	(171)
About right	68.4	66.4	67.4
(Number)	(475)	(448)	(923)
Too few blacks	18.7	21.5	20.1
(Number)	(130)	(145)	(275)
Totals[b]	99.9	100.0	100.0
(Number)	(694)	(675)	(1,369)

[a]See text for actual wording of questions.

[b]"Don't know" and "no answer" responses (201 cases) have been excluded.

Source: 1982 National Opinion Research Center General Social Survey (N = 1,570).Table 9-2

those respondents may have as much to do with the supposed "problem" as does the military census itself.

Demographic Characteristics

The usual breakdowns of respondents by race, sex, and marital status provide some insights into the people questioned and the answers they gave; but except for race, those categories showed no particular correlation with attitudes toward blacks in the military. To develop a more enlightening analysis, then, we will also look at the respondents according to (a) their membership in synthetic groups called age cohorts, and (b) their affluence.

The members of an age cohort are people who are approximately the same age and have presumably had many common experiences. The cohort groups are—

World War I Cohort—Born before 1906, these respondents were at least 10 years old in 1916 and at least 76 years old in 1982.

Depression Cohort—These respondents reached age 21 between 1928 and 1944 and were 59-75 years old in 1982.

World War II Cohort—These respondents reached age 21 between 1945 and 1960 and were 43-58 years old in 1982.

Vietnam Cohort—These respondents became adults (for some, this meant turning 18) between 1961 and 1974 and were 26-42 years old in 1982.

Watergate Cohort—These respondents started turning 18 in 1975 and were between 18 and 25 in 1982.

Each of these cohorts covers an age range of from 15 to 17 years. They do not contain the same number of respondents, because members of older cohorts have higher mortality rates and the youngest cohort has yet to be completely filled.[2]

We look at the affluence of the respondents because it has been established that social class is inversely related to confidence in the military.[3] The respondents were divided into two broad groups: those living in families whose household incomes are less than $25,000 per year, and those living in families whose household incomes are $25,000 or more per year.

> *Whereas a large majority of whites think that the number of blacks in uniform is about right, opinion among blacks is more divided.*

Table 9-2 presents the breakdowns by race, sex, marital status, age cohort, and affluence. We see that blacks are more concerned than whites about the high percentage of blacks in the armed services. At the same time, more blacks than whites think there are too few blacks in the military. In short, whereas a large majority of whites think that the number of blacks in uniform is about right, opinion among blacks is more divided.

Sex and marital status show little correlation with attitudes toward blacks in the military. Membership in an age cohort also shows little correlation. Perhaps so few people are dissatisfied with the number of

Table 9-2

Relationship Between Demographic Characteristics and Concern About Blacks in the Military

Demographic Characteristic	Too Many Blacks	About Right	Too Few Blacks	Total No. of Respondents[a]
Race				
White	11.0%	70.8%	18.1%	1,169
Black	21.0	47.5	31.5	200
Sex				
Male	16.9	63.8	19.3	585
Female	9.2	70.2	20.7	784
Marital Status				
Single	11.7	64.4	23.8	239
Married	12.8	68.9	18.3	792
Other	12.4	66.0	21.6	338
Age Cohort				
WW I	9.6	69.9	20.5	83
Depression	10.5	66.1	23.5	277
WW II	16.1	65.5	18.4	304
Vietnam	14.3	66.9	18.8	489
Watergate	7.0	71.8	21.1	213
Family Income				
Less than $25,000/year	10.2	67.7	22.0	898
$25,000/year or more	15.9	68.6	15.4	370

[a] "Don't know" and "no answer" responses have been excluded.

Source: 1982 National Opinion Research Center General Social Survey (N = 1,570).

blacks in the military that there is little room for variation from one age group to the next.

The responses of the two income cohorts are likewise roughly similar, and they, too, show no particular correlation with attitudes toward blacks in the military. But when we look only at respondents in the "too many" category, a more interesting result becomes clear. Although respondents from households with incomes of $25,000 or more are only about 30 percent of the total survey population, they constitute almost 40 percent of those who think there are too many blacks in the military. (The upper-income group would include the nation's agenda-setters: political leaders, social commentators, scholars, and professionals.) Their influence may have been crucial in generating the appearance of public concern even when evidence shows little actual concern.

Political and Social Characteristics

Although attitudes toward the military and toward racial issues often vary with party identification, among the 1982 GSS respondents there is no relationship between party identification and views on blacks in the military. The percentages of Republicans, Independents, and Democrats are statistically similar in each category of attitudes toward blacks in the military (table 9-3).

Measuring respondents' attitudes toward blacks in the military against a scale of attitudes toward school desegregation, however, yields a somewhat more telling picture (table 9-3). The measure of school desegregation was used because it has been demonstrated to be a good measure of racial tolerance in general.[4] In addition, the assumption that a person's level of racial tolerance might bear directly on that person's attitude toward blacks in the military seems a logical one to make.

The scale of racial tolerance used here is the Guttman scale, which produces a score on the basis of the pattern of responses to a series of questions. In this case, the questions were—

The patterns of response in the three categories of attitude toward blacks in the military do not differ significantly from one category of tolerance to another.

A. Would you yourself have any objection to sending your children to a school where a few of the children were blacks/whites?

B. *If not intolerant on A:* Would you yourself have any objection to sending your children to a school where half of the children were blacks/whites?

C. *If not intolerant on B:* Would you yourself have any objection to sending your children to a school where most of the children were blacks/whites?

Whites were asked the questions in terms of blacks, and blacks in terms of whites. A positive response to

Table 9-3
Relationship Between Political and Social Attitudes and Concern About Blacks in the Military

Political/Social Attitude	Too Many Blacks	About Right	Too Few Blacks	Total No. of Respondents[a]
Party Identification				
Republicans	10.9%	69.6%	19.5%	303
Independents	12.7	70.3	17.1	498
Democrats	13.1	63.7	23.2	557
Tolerance of School Desegregation				
Most intolerant	19.7	52.1	28.2	71
Somewhat intolerant	15.9	67.8	16.4	214
Somewhat tolerant	10.3	72.6	17.1	387
Most tolerant	12.0	64.9	23.1	619

[a]"Don't know" and "no answer" responses have been excluded.

Source: 1982 National Opinion Research Center General Social Survey (N = 1,570).

part A resulted in the "most intolerant" score on the scale. A negative response to part A but a positive response to part B resulted in a "somewhat intolerant" score on the scale, and so on. Unlike most survey questions on race relations, this one is applicable to both blacks and whites.

The patterns of response in the three categories of attitude toward blacks in the military do not differ significantly from one category of tolerance to another. The 19.7 percent of the most intolerant respondents who think that the military services are too black is somewhat above the overall rate (table 9-1) of 12.5 percent. Only 71 respondents are found in this category, however, and the difference between 19.7 percent and 12.5 percent is not statistically significant. Similarly, the difference between the somewhat intolerant group (15.9 percent—214 respondents) and the overall distribution (12.5 percent) merely borders on statistical significance.

But if race makes a difference in whether or not people think there are too many blacks in the military (and we see from table 9-2 that it does), and if blacks and whites are known to differ significantly on racial tolerance,[5] then the responses of blacks and whites may show significantly different relationships between attitudes toward blacks in the military and racial tolerance. When whites alone are examined (not shown), a disproportionately large fraction of those who think there are too many blacks in the services are either most intolerant or somewhat intolerant. But since only 5.1 percent of white respondents are "most intolerant" and less than 18 percent are "somewhat intolerant," people in these categories are overrepresented (10 percent and 27.5 percent, respectively) among whites who say that there are too many blacks in the military. The tolerance scale is not as revealing of the attitudes of blacks, since all blacks in the 1982 GSS scored somewhat tolerant or most tolerant (not shown).

Attitudes on Military Issues

The 1982 GSS asked several questions on other kinds of military matters and related the distribution of respondents' opinions on those other military matters to their attitudes on blacks in the armed services (table 9-4).

Only 3 percent of the respondents to the survey believed there were too many blacks in the service and lacked confidence in the military; and only 2.5 percent of those surveyed believed that the military is too black and that the quality of military personnel is poor.

Respondents were asked whether they thought the amount of federal spending on the military was "too much," "too little," or "about right." Regardless of their attitudes toward military spending, most respondents still felt that the percentage of blacks in the military was "about right." There was also no relationship between feelings on military spending and the belief that the military had "too many" or "too few" blacks.

Respondents were also asked how much confidence they had in "the people running" the armed services. Possible responses were "a great deal of confidence," "only some confidence," and "hardly any confidence at all." Only 201 of the survey respondents answering this question, or about 15 percent, had a great deal of confidence in the military. This level of confidence is far higher than the confidence these same respondents placed in some other institutions, but it is not very high.

120

Table 9-4

Relationship Between Attitudes on Military Issues and Concern About Blacks in the Military

Military Issue	Too Many Blacks	About Right	Too Few Blacks	Total No. of Respondents[a]
Military Spending				
Too little	10.5%	68.7%	20.8%	399
About right	11.6	71.8	16.5	490
Too much	15.5	63.0	21.5	414
Confidence in Military				
Great deal	22.4	60.2	17.4	201
Some	11.5	68.4	20.1	703
Not much	9.9	69.6	20.5	415
Quality of Military Personnel				
Poor	24.6	53.6	21.7	138
Not so good	16.0	67.2	16.9	445
Good	8.2	70.4	21.4	635
Excellent	7.1	67.1	25.9	85

[a]"Don't know" and "no answer" responses have been excluded.
Source: 1982 National Opinion Research Center General Social Survey (N = 1,570).

Finally, respondents were asked to rate the overall quality of military personnel as "excellent," "good," "not so good," or "poor." Almost half of those surveyed did not have a good opinion of the quality of military personnel: some 10.6 percent (138) said "poor" and another 34.2 percent (445) said "not so good."

If we were to discover that the responses to the questions on confidence and quality were related to views on blacks in the military, we could then conclude that the high percentage of blacks might actually be diminishing the public's confidence in national security.

Table 9-4 shows that there is not much relationship between people's attitudes toward military spending and their views on blacks in the military. Only 3 percent of the respondents to the survey believed there were too many blacks in the service *and* lacked confidence in the military; and only 2.5 percent of those surveyed believed that the military is too black *and* that the quality of military personnel is poor. Looked at another way, more than 22 percent (45 respondents) of those having a great deal of confidence in the military think there are too many blacks in the services; and more than a quarter of the respondents who think that the services are too black (171, see table 9-1) have a great deal of confidence in the military. (It should be kept in mind that only about 15 percent of the overall survey population has such high confidence). Thus, what little concern there is about the disproportionate number of blacks in the armed services is not undermining confidence in the military.

On the basis of these public opinion data, concern over the number of blacks in the military is unwarranted and may serve only to deflect attention from more important issues about public confidence in the military.

The difference between the racial composition of the military and that of the society from which it draws its ranks has been pronounced a problem by some people. They believe that black overrepresentation undermines the public support necessary to a military establishment that is charged with protecting the nation's global interests. Opinion research shows, however, that the public, or at least the white part of it, is by and large content to have 20 percent of the military and 30 percent of the army be black. Whites who are dissatisfied with those percentages constitute a slender minority, within which the affluent, the racially intolerant, those concerned about the quality of military personnel, and those "gung-ho" with confidence in the military are overrepresented. Blacks as a group show a higher rate of concern, but the preponderance of black respondents is satisfied with the current level of representation.

Although the public tends to express confidence in our military establishment, a significant minority (almost a third) does not have much confidence; and almost half of those surveyed also have qualms about the quality of America's military personnel. But in the mind of the public, neither of these issues is linked to the number of blacks in the military. On the basis of these public opinion data, therefore, concern over the number of blacks in the military is unwarranted and may serve only to deflect attention from more important issues about public confidence in the military.

Attitudes Toward Women in the Military

The 1982 General Social Survey also included a number of questions on women and the military. Only about 8 percent of the respondents answered that there were too many women in the military; less than 15 percent thought there were too few; and the rest (77 percent) were satisfied with the sexual makeup of the armed services. Apparently, then, the public is not concerned about the number of women in the military.

However, two perennial questions about women in the military merit examination. One is whether women, like men, should be compelled to serve if the nation reinstitutes some form of compulsory national service. The other, of more immediate consequence for military personnel policy, has to do with the roles women play in the armed forces: how, for example, does the public feel about the combat-exclusion policy that Lawrence Korb discusses in chapter 3?

The 1982 GSS asked several questions on a draft, including separate questions about drafting men and drafting women. With an identical question pertaining to men placed immediately before or after it, the question on drafting women was worded as follows:

> How would you feel about a program that required all young women to give one year of service to the nation—either in the military forces or in non-military work such as in hospitals or with elderly people? Would you strongly favor it, probably favor it, probably oppose it, or strongly oppose it?

Obviously, this question allows for the possibility of service other than military service, but military service is strongly implied. The *procedure* in question is a draft; and in the United States all previous drafts have been designed to compel military service. Moreover, the results obtained in the 1982 GSS (table 9-5) coincide with the responses to previous surveys and reinforce our interpretation that respondents had a military draft in mind when they answered this question.

About 8 percent of the respondents answered that there were too many women in the military; less than 15 percent thought there were too few; and the rest (77 percent) were satisfied with the sexual makeup of the armed services.

Table 9-5

Attitudes About Requiring National Service From Women

	Percent	Number
Strongly favor	26.6	396
Probably favor	36.2	541
Probably oppose	21.6	323
Strongly oppose	15.6	233
Total[a]	100.0	1,493

[a]"Don't know" and "no answer" responses have been excluded.

Source: 1982 National Opinion Research Center General Social Survey (N = 1,570).

The figures presented in table 9-5 are fairly compelling. Nearly 63 percent of the respondents said they would favor including women if the nation had a required program of national service.

Demographic Characteristics

Few demographic characteristics distinguish those favoring required service for women. The distribution of responses among groups by race and sex (table 9-6), for example, is very similar to the distribution among the total survey population (table 9-5). Whether black or white, male or female, respondents showed the same solid support for the concept of drafting women. Support was also strong in all categories of marital status—single, married, and formerly married.

There are, however, some slight and surprising age-cohort differences in attitudes toward drafting women. The percentage of World War I cohort members (all of whom were at least 76 years old in 1982) who favor drafting women was slightly greater than the percentage in the total population. Of the 94 World War I cohort members surveyed, 38.3 percent strongly favored drafting women and 26.6 percent said they would probably favor it, for a total of 64.9 percent (compared with 26.6 and 36.2 percent, respectively, in the general population, for a total of

Table 9-6
Relationship Between Demographic Characteristics and Attitudes About Requiring National Service From Women

Demographic Characteristic	Strongly Favor	Probably Favor	Probably Oppose	Strongly Oppose	Total No. of Respondents[a]
Race					
White	27.1%	35.6%	22.4%	14.9%	1,274
Black	23.6	40.2	16.9	19.6	219
Sex					
Male	30.0	31.7	22.2	16.0	630
Female	24.0	39.5	21.2	15.3	863
Marital Status					
Single	22.6	37.4	24.5	15.6	257
Married	27.1	36.1	22.4	14.3	855
Other	27.8	35.7	18.1	18.4	392
Age-Cohort Membership					
WW I	38.3	26.6	20.2	14.9	94
Depression	36.5	30.9	16.6	16.0	307
WW II	26.0	34.2	22.5	17.3	242
Vietnam	23.7	43.3	20.6	12.5	520
Watergate	14.7	35.3	30.8	19.2	224
Family Income					
Less than $25,000/year	26.8	36.6	20.2	16.4	959
$25,000/year or more	26.3	37.7	24.6	11.4	411

[a]"Don't know" and "no answer" responses have been excluded.

Source: 1982 National Opinion Research Center General Social Survey (N = 1,570).

62.8 percent). Still, the World War I cohort is just 6.3 percent of the total survey population; even its enthusiastic support does not account for the popularity of the idea.

In contrast, the youngest cohort displays considerably less "very strong" support for the idea of drafting females (14.7 percent). Although the Watergate cohort constituted a little more than 15 percent of the nation's total population in 1982, it makes up only 8.4 percent of those who back drafting females most strongly. Quite possibly, this group is simply more anti-draft than other cohorts. After all, it is the only cohort with members of draft age.

The last of the demographic characteristics—social class (as measured by family income)—does not correlate with attitudes toward requiring national service for women. The distributions for both the more and the less affluent are unremarkable. It seems, then, that there is considerable broad-based support for drafting women into military service.

Political and Social Characteristics

One might expect party identification to be related to attitudes toward drafting women, especially given the opposing stands the two major parties took during the 1980 presidential election on passage of the Equal Rights Amendment. This, however, is not the case. Democrats, Independents, and Republicans all show similar degrees of support for and opposition to programs of national service that include women. The distribution of opinions within each political affiliation is statistically similar to the distribution within the total survey population.

Although at this point the investigation might logically turn to the relationship between views on drafting women and attitudes toward feminism, no scale for measuring those attitudes has been shown to have the reliability of the Guttman racial tolerance scale. The GSS does pose some questions on women's issues, but none is appropriate for our purposes. Rather than rely on an incomplete or biased measure, we employ the scale on racial tolerance because racial views and attitudes on feminist issues have been demonstrated to be closely correlated.[6]

Table 9-7 shows that there is some relationship between racial intolerance and attitudes toward requiring women to serve in the military. A relatively small percentage of the most intolerant respondents "probably favor" drafting females, and a relatively large percentage of them definitely oppose the procedure. Even though the most intolerant make up only 6 percent of the population, their high rate of strong opposition makes them significant.

Democrats, Independents, and Republicans all show similar degrees of support for and opposition to programs of national service that include women.

126

Table 9-7

Relationship Between Political and Social Attitudes and Attitudes About Requiring National Service From Women

Political/Social Attitude	Strongly Favor	Probably Favor	Probably Oppose	Strongly Oppose	Total No. of Respondents[a]
Party Identification					
Republicans	26.7%	36.2%	22.7%	14.4%	326
Independents	25.0	36.8	22.0	16.2	536
Democrats	27.6	35.9	20.8	15.6	615
Tolerance of School Desegregation					
Most intolerant	33.3	22.6	16.7	27.4	84
Somewhat intolerant	27.0	38.9	19.9	14.2	226
Somewhat tolerant	24.8	35.0	26.5	13.8	412
Most tolerant	26.1	37.1	20.6	16.2	685

[a]"Don't know" and "no answer" responses have been excluded.

Source: 1982 National Opinion Research Center General Social Survey (N = 1,570).

Attitudes on Military Issues

Of the three military issues (military spending, confidence in the military establishment, and quality of military personnel), attitudes on two—spending and confidence—turn out not to be associated with views on drafting women for military duty (table 9-8). Regardless of what the survey respondents think about the level of military spending, their views on requiring service from women have the same distribution as the views of the total survey population. Similarly, the survey reveals no differences on this issue between the total population and the respondents who have a great deal, only some, or not much confidence in the military. Members of all groups generally favor or oppose the conscription of women to the same extent.

But attitudes on the quality of military personnel do bear some slight relationship to opinions about requiring national service from women. First, although 36.2 percent of the total population "probably favors" drafting women (table 9-5), only 26.8

127

Table 9-8

Relationship Between Attitudes on Military Issues and Attitudes About Requiring National Service From Women

Military Issue	Strongly Favor	Probably Favor	Probably Oppose	Strongly Oppose	Total No. of Respondents[a]
Military Spending					
Too little	28.8%	33.9%	23.2%	14.2%	431
About right	26.9	38.1	21.8	13.3	528
Too much	24.1	35.8	21.0	19.0	452
Confidence in Military					
Great deal	24.5	31.5	21.4	18.6	220
Some	23.8	38.8	22.6	14.9	800
Not much	31.9	33.0	20.2	14.8	445
Quality of Military Personnel					
Poor	32.2	26.8	18.1	22.8	149
Not so good	25.3	37.7	24.7	12.3	486
Good	23.1	40.6	22.6	13.7	672
Excellent	47.2	20.2	12.4	20.2	89

[a]"Don't know" and "no answer" responses have been excluded.

Source: 1982 National Opinion Research Center General Social Survey (N = 1,570).

percent of those having the lowest opinion of our troops answer in that way. Second, among respondents who hold the personnel of the armed forces in the highest regard, fewer are "probably opposed" to drafting women than is the case in the overall population (12.4 in contrast to 21.6 percent). Further, those who think America's troops are excellent are more strongly in favor of drafting women than is the overall population (47.2 and 26.6 percent, respectively). It seems, then, that those who think highly of military personnel are more in favor of drafting women, whereas those who think the least of our personnel are less in favor of it. This all must be taken with some reservation, however, since the two extreme positions on the quality of military personnel constitute a total of only 17.1 percent of the survey respondents. In short, this relationship should be considered weakly significant.

Table 9-9

Public Acceptance of Roles for Women in the Military

Military Role	Public Acceptance
Typist in the Pentagon	97%
Nurse in a combat zone	94
Truck mechanic	83
Jet transport pilot	73
Jet fighter pilot	62
Commander of a large military base	62
Air defense missile gunner	60
Crew member on a combat ship	58
Soldier in hand-to-hand combat	31

Source: 1982 National Opinion Research Center General Social Survey (N = 1,570).

The Role of Women in the Armed Forces

The 1982 GSS also asked its respondents several questions about the role of women in the armed forces. Those interviewed were asked about several military jobs and whether or not they thought a woman should be allowed to serve in each one, "assuming she is trained to do it." The results show that there is very little the public is unwilling to allow women in the military to do (table 9-9). Although only a little less than a third of the respondents want to see women in hand-to-hand combat, that is still a large number. Giving servicewomen other duty stations with a high potential for combat as well as command over men is approved of by a substantial majority of all respondents.

The highest approval rates (more than 90 percent) are for jobs that women in the military have traditionally performed—typist and nurse. However, clear majorities of the public would approve of women's doing jobs from which they are now excluded; 58 percent would favor women's serving on combat ships, and 62 percent would allow women to fly jet fighters.

It would appear, then, that the armed services' combat-exclusion policy is more restrictive than public opinion would justify. One must keep in mind, however, that these answers were obtained during a period when the nation was not at war. The responses might change if the possibility of women's actually seeing combat were imminent.

Conclusion

What lessons can we draw from this inquiry? First, we know now that there simply is not very much public concern over the racial composition of the military. The dissatisfaction that does exist seems to trouble blacks more than whites; but many blacks favor greater black representation, not less. In fact, in both races, more people favor increasing the percentage of blacks than favor decreasing it. In addition, widespread support exists for equalizing men's and women's responsibility to serve in the military.

We have also learned that the public's confidence in the military has not been eroded by the high percentages of blacks in the military. Only tiny fractions of respondents have *both* negative attitudes toward the overrepresentation of blacks in the armed forces and negative attitudes on other military issues. Similarly, the drafting of women would have little effect on public confidence in the military or on the public's perception of the quality of military personnel. Neither the disproportionate presence of blacks within the military nor the potential need to use women to meet force levels in periods of rapid mobilization has any effect on the esteem in which military institutions are held. Yet, even though the military continues to produce a feeling of security in most people, a substantial portion of Americans believe the military is not as good as it should be. What this study shows profoundly is that the source of their concern is not the racial or sexual composition of our troops.

What lessons can we draw from this inquiry? . . . That there simply is not very much public concern over the racial composition of the military . . . [and] in fact, in both races, more people favor increasing the percentage of blacks than favor decreasing it.

Endnotes

1. Morris Janowitz, *The Last Half-Century: Societal Change and Politics in America* (Chicago: University of Chicago Press, 1978).

2. A. Wade Smith, "Racial Tolerance as a Function of Group Position," *American Sociological Review* 46:5 (1981): 558-573; A. Wade Smith, "Public Consciousness of Blacks in the Military," *Journal of Political and Military Sociology* 1:2 (1983): 281-300.

3. A. Wade Smith, "Public Consciousness"; A. Wade Smith, "Social Class and Racial Cleavages on Major Social Indicators," *Research in Racial and Ethnic Relations* 4 (1985): 33-65.

4. Smith, "Public Consciousness"; Smith, "Racial Tolerance."

5. Gunnar Myrdal, *An American Dilemma* (New York: Harper and Row, 1944, rpt. 1962); A. Wade Smith, "Social Class."

6. Robert S. Erikson, N. R. Luttbeg, and K. L. Tedin, *American Public Opinion: Its Origin, Content, and Impact* (New York: John Wiley and Sons, 1980).

10. LESSONS FROM OTHER TIMES, OTHER PLACES

Cynthia H. Enloe

J ust after dawn, the troops marched on board in a colorful scene: the Scots Guards, to the skirl of a piper playing "Scotland and Brave"; Welsh Guards, with their band blaring out "Men of Harlech"; and rugged Gurkhas, all volunteers from Nepal, to the accompaniment of Hindu prayers.[1]

It seems like a scene from Kipling: a Victorian British force setting out to preserve the queen's imperial glory, using soldiers from ethnic groups already made subject to English rule. We tend to associate such ethnically distinct military units with a bygone era. They seem remote from modern military forces with their sophisticated managerial controls, computers, and jet aircraft.

In fact, this scene, so colorfully described by a *New York Times* reporter, took place in 1982 when Britain fought Argentina over the Falkland Islands. The Scottish, Welsh, and Gurkha troops were setting sail aboard a hastily re-outfitted *Queen Elizabeth II* to join one of the largest, most sophisticated naval and air task forces launched in recent decades. The ethnic delineations of the British Falklands task force are as contemporary as the expensive weaponry the force carried with it.

The British are not alone in continuing to use ethnic identities and racial categories self-consciously as bases for recruiting and deploying military manpower. There is scarcely a military force in the world today whose ethnic or racial composition is either representative of the ethnic or racial composition of its civilian population or completely random.[2]

The representativeness of a military force's manpower and the self-consciousness with which a

There is scarcely a military force in the world today whose ethnic or racial composition is either representative of the ethnic or racial composition of its civilian population or completely random.

government manipulates ethnic and racial identities in recruiting and deploying troops can become hotly debated political issues at specific points in a country's history. Usually, however, questions about the ethnic or racial composition of the military lie below the political surface, apparently not at issue.

It is important to clarify the degree of conscious policy-making at the root of any military force's ethnic or racial structure: when and how do officials *not* leave the composition of the navy, army, or air force to chance? It is also important to determine the circumstances under which the make-up of the troops and of the officer corps becomes a matter of public scrutiny and debate. The ethnic or racial composition of the military and the extent of its political "visibility" will shape the ways in which a government will try to use its military forces. In addition, the strategies a government tries to use—not always with success—will be shaped in part by the sorts of resources it has; and that, in turn, will depend on how rich the government is, how literate its people have become, and how much of its weaponry it produces or has to import. Finally and perhaps less obviously, the military-ethnic dynamics in each country will be affected by the relations between women and men and between women and governing elites in that country.

Ethnic groups—in or out of power—are not monolithic. They are usually divided by class and by gender. Women in an ethnic community typically are excluded from political influence and from military service; but women have their own values and their own strategies, and these can shape the military outlooks of their brothers, sons, husbands, and workmates. How an ethnically or racially anxious government tries to use men of different ethnic groups will depend in part on which group has women whom the government imagines it can use militarily. As in the politics of health and the politics of industry, so too in the politics of militaries, race, ethnicity, and sex are intimately woven together with the inequities of power. All of that together—race, ethnicity, sex, and their roles in the dynamics of power—determine which groups in a country will feel secure and which insecure as a result of any military deployment abroad or at home.

The ethnic or racial composition of the military and the extent of its political "visibility" will shape the ways in which a government will try to use its military forces.

Ethnically Divided Militaries in Preindustrial Countries

Watching the Gurkha men go up the gangplank of the *Queen Elizabeth II* on their way to the Falklands evoked images of pre-industrial military forces, forces that relied heavily on mercenaries or forced labor and that were not rooted in popularly supported political systems. Before the Industrial Revolution and the rise of the concept of the popular democratic state, officials deliberately designed their military forces to implement the government's larger divide-and-rule governing formulas. Hardly a military force in the world mirrored the population it was allegedly defending. In fact, governmental elites were often themselves foreigners ruling far from home or members of local but small racial or ethnic minorities that had gained dominance by controlling land, weapons, or trade routes. Those elites were afraid to enlist men from all sectors of the general populace. Such forces would be likely either to mutiny or to join popular nationalist revolutions to oust the foreign or minority rulers.

[Before the industrial revolution], hardly a military force in the world mirrored the population it was allegedly defending.

The larger the state and the more expansive its territorial aspirations, the more likely its ruling elite was to implement a deliberate calculus of military manpower based on an ethnic or racial divide-and-rule principle.[3] For instance, the Indian peoples of what is now Latin America were conquered and then ruled by light-complexioned Spanish troops. Only later were darker complexioned Indian men conscripted into the Spanish Latin American forces, and they were always kept in the lower ranks and never really trusted. That history has its parallel in the 1980s, when the internal politics (and coup dynamics) of every Andean country's military are affected by the differentiations among the hispanicized white elites, the upwardly mobile mestizo officers, and the Indio rank and file.[4]

Similarly, the British colonial rulers in India repeatedly revised their ethnic calculations to dominate that ethnically diverse region. After the famous Mutiny of 1857, for instance, British administrators decided that Hindus were not a "martial race" after

135

all—"martial race" being a racist formula that English recruiters had already elaborated when trying to enlist Scotsmen back home in Britain.[5] Instead, Gurkhas, an ethnic group from what is now Nepal, Muslims from the Punjab, and Sikhs from northern India were held up by British officials as models of the "martial races."

This notion—that the men of some ethnic or racial groups are "naturally" suited to military occupations—often has little to do with ethnographic analysis.

This notion—that the men of some ethnic or racial groups are "naturally" suited to military occupations—often has little to do with ethnographic analysis. It has far more to do with whom the senior government officials believe they can trust and who can be persuaded to join and stay in the military in large enough numbers to support the regime against foreign and domestic challenges.

Most pre-twentieth-century military manpower strategists seem to have considered three factors simultaneously in attempting to build military forces that would serve the purposes of the central government. The three factors are availability, competence, and political reliability.

Availability. The ethnic or racial groups whose political and educational status made them most attractive to military manpower strategists often did not have enough adult men to fill the ranks. Or men from the "desirable" groups might have rejected military service, preferring instead to devote their energies to farming, commerce, or careers in the state's civilian bureaucracy. Beliefs about manliness and about soldiering do not bolster each other in every culture. Consequently, the availability of men from any particular ethnic group was determined in large measure by the conditions affecting, and options open to, the particular group.

Those conditions and options were not constant. Many ethnic groups' fortunes have waxed and waned at different points in history. Unemployment is not a fixed condition, and the means of gaining capital for commerce, of becoming a landowner, or of winning a place within the government's civil service also vary for men of different ethnic or racial groups at different times. An ethnic group that disdains a military career in one era and whose men are less "available" to military recruiters may later look to the military as

136

an attractive alternative because that group has lost access to jobs elsewhere or because the military has acquired new social prestige and economic resources. Even if women of a community are not the targets of military recruiting, their ideas about what constitutes a "decent job" or a "respectable career" will help shape their sons' and husbands' attitudes toward military enlistment.

Competence. The second criterion that most governments used (and still use) in attempting to build military forces that would serve the central government's own purpose is military competence. In pre-industrial military forces, competence did not always require that soldiers be fluent in the official language of the country. Many ethnic groups whose male members had only a limited degree of fluency in the language that the government elite used for military operations were nonetheless considered "natural warriors." In fact, military "competence" was often reduced to racist stereotypes. Groups famed for being "martial races"—that is, for some-how having males born with a proclivity for organized violence—include Scottish Highlanders, Cossacks, Nepalese Gurkhas, Sikhs, Berbers of North Africa, North American Sioux, Zulus of southern Africa, Prussians, and Montenegrins from what is now Yugoslavia.

What they shared, however, was not genes but historical and social conditions that placed them on the margins of state systems (Prussians, who occupied a dominant position among the German states, were an exception). They often lived along trade routes where they were constantly in the middle of conflicts between larger states; or they lived in regions where young men had little opportunity for agricultural labor or cash employment.

Presumptions about military competence not only shaped who was recruited for and excluded from a given military force; they also determined where the men of various ethnic groups were concentrated inside the military. Military forces, even before the technological explosion of the 19th century in the conduct of warfare, were complex organizations, and a country's ethnic or racial division of labor was usually replicated within its military (as within its

Presumptions about military competence not only shaped who was recruited for and excluded from a given military force; they also determined where the men of various ethnic groups were concentrated inside the military.

schools, workshops, civil service, and plantations). The men of some ethnic groups were officially presumed to be effective in the ranks but unfit for the officer corps; some were alleged to be especially good horsemen, while others were considered skilled with the crossbow; some groups were thought to produce natural trackers, whereas others gained a reputation for being especially valuable as sailors. Many of these presumptions never died out. They became myths, living well beyond the technologies that inspired them. These myths persist even now, so that military organization still reflects the stratified division of labor in the larger society and still helps to sustain the social hierarchy, especially in countries where the military has substantial political influence.

Political reliability. The third criterion that governments used (and use) in their recruiting calculations is political reliability. In a governmental elite's best-of-all-worlds, the group perceived to have the greatest natural military competence would also be available for military service in adequate numbers to serve the existing security strategy and it would display such strong loyalty to the high command and the government that it could be trusted to use its weapons and skills to serve rather than oppose the state. This ideal situation rarely existed. The further removed the reality was (in the eyes of officials) from the ideal, the more likely it was that manpower policy would be fraught with ethnic or racial calculations.

Governments used all sorts of analytical formulas and concepts—geographic region, generation, sex, and economic class—to predict political reliability, but probably no concept was used more by governments than ethnicity.

Governments used all sorts of analytical formulas and concepts—geographic region, generation, sex, and economic class—to predict political reliability, but probably no concept was used more by governments than ethnicity. British and French colonial administrators even hired ethnographers to predict which groups would ally themselves with the colonial regime, which would passively resist its administration, and which would openly challenge it. Even today, ethnography and anthropology can be tools in the hands of military strategists at home and abroad. Central governments and field commanders are eager to find ways of predicting the behavior of the people under their jurisdiction.

Like military availability and competence, political loyalty was—and is—historically specific,

138

not fixed once and for all. For example, a new government coming to power and needing new allies sometimes makes deliberate overtures to a formerly alienated group, offering to improve the group's military status. Likewise, it is often not until late in a war that a government's efforts to juggle availability, competence, and political reliability become most transparent: once a war has dragged on far longer than the government had originally anticipated and casualties are putting a great strain on the preferred pools of manpower, military commanders tentatively start to calculate the risks of recruiting men from ethnic groups that, at the beginning of the war, were excluded because officials did not trust them. A story is told about a Burmese monarch who, after continual warring against surrounding Asian kingdoms, was so desperate for troops that he began conscripting men from politically alienated ethnic minorities. He sent them into battle chained together.[6] The account may be apocryphal, but it depicts *in extremis* the less dramatic but politically significant dilemmas experienced by English-speaking commanders of French-Canadian forces late in World War I, by the white commanders of Rhodesia's army late in its war against African liberation forces in the 1970s, and by white South African military strategists in the 1980s.

> *Even today, ethnography and anthropology can be tools in the hands of military strategists at home and abroad.*

Ethnic Divisions Within Modern Militaries

It is commonly taken for granted that with modernization comes the decline of ethnic identity. The modern person, it is assumed, will think of himself or herself as an autonomous individual, making choices on the basis of individual options and identifying himself or herself as the citizen of a central state. According to this view, ethnicity will fade over time, not only in social interactions and economic transactions but also in the construction and structure of military forces. Of course, as we know, this projection has proved sadly inadequate as a description of the status of ethnicity not only in twentieth-century American society but also in other industrialized and urbanized societies such as Canada, France, Germany, Belgium, and the Soviet Union.

Instead, what has happened is that ethnic and racial formulas of military manpower, like weaponry and strategic theory, have been modernized. However, it has become far riskier than it once was for military manpower strategists to *admit* that they consciously take ethnic or racial identities into account when they recruit, assign, and deploy their forces. This risk arises because modern states and their militaries depend for their legitimacy and popular support on another myth—the myth that they represent society as a whole. But despite this second myth, the modernization that has so radically escalated the destructive potential of military forces has made ethnicity not less, but more, important. In the eyes of governments, the composition of the nuclear- or laser-equipped military is too important to be left to chance.

> *The modernization that has so radically escalated the destructive potential of military forces has made ethnicity not less, but more, important.*

We can test this proposition by looking at the Soviet Union, whose military is a prime example of a rapidly modernizing force. Since the Bolshevik Revolution, and particularly since World War II, the Soviet leadership has invested increasingly in the modernization of its military. Today that force commands technological and scientific resources matched only by those of the United States. If modernization means the demise of the military importance of ethnicity, therefore, one would expect the current Soviet military command structure to be preoccupied with the latest in tank technology and nuclear strategies, not with the changing ethnic composition of the Red Army's rank and file. But this is not the case. Soviet military strategists think ethnically. They think ethnically because the entire Soviet national security policy is predicated on the assimilation of all other ethnic groups into Russian culture.

To the Soviet leadership, assimilation means that the "ideal" Soviet citizen would speak Russian, accept Russian cultural values, and so on. Assimilation into Russian culture is to be distinguished from Russian chauvinism, which denotes a set of attitudes and actions that causes ethnic Russians to view their group as superior to other groups and leads them to reject other groups' cultural values and to exclude members of other groups from prominent positions.

Russian chauvinism has been loudly condemned by the Communist party leadership, which has pursued policies aimed at unifying the country's diverse population. Nevertheless, since 1917 as under the czars, the country's government has been dominated by men from the ethnic Russian community plus a smattering of white Slavs.

But despite the party's condemnation of Russian chauvinism, considerable alienation has persisted among non-Russian Soviet citizens. They resent what they see as deliberate government efforts to "Russify" their young people, to make their cultures marginal, and to reserve the privileges of power for the most trusted group—the Russians. In that context, ethnic population projections have political meaning.

In the Soviet military, as in other areas of Soviet life, the effort of assimilation has been integral to Soviet leaders' notion of modernization.[7] National security is measured in part by the success the Red Army has in assimilating non-Russian men. Consequently, ethnicity continues to have great relevance for the Soviet military, not despite but because of that military's level of modernization.[8]

Soviet military strategists think ethnically especially when they consider the army because it is the army, more than the Soviet navy or air force, that depends on large numbers of male conscripts (less than 1 percent of the army are women). The army is therefore very sensitive to changes in birth rates among the Soviet Union's several ethnic groups. Currently, ethnic Russians make up most of the officer corps of the Red Army, according to foreign analysts. Asian Soviet conscripts are likely to be assigned to construction units because of their lack of facility in the Russian language.[9]

Every time a census is taken, nervous tremors run through Moscow's national security hierarchy. The Red Army's pool of conscripts is changing as ethnic Russian women have fewer children and Asian Soviet women have large families. Since 1917, the proportion of ethnic Russians in Soviet society has been slipping. The 1980 census revealed that ethnic Russians constituted just over 50 percent of the

In the Soviet military, as in other areas of Soviet life, the effort of assimilation has been integral to Soviet leaders' notion of modernization.

Soviet population. Some observers predict that if the ethnically divergent birth rates persist, by the year 2000, of all conscripts in the Soviet army, 33 percent will be Uzbeks, Kazakhs, and other Asian men.

In certain situations, Soviet leadership recognizes that ethnic distinctions may be convenient. Apparently the government deliberately used mainly Asian Soviet units in its initial advance into Afghanistan, probably hoping that such a force would be viewed more favorably than heavily Russian units would be. The government later withdrew those troops because some of them sympathized with Afghan fellow-Muslims. This suggests the degree to which Soviet military policy rides on ethnic calculations of manpower and also the degree to which the calculations may be wrong.

The Indonesian experience suggests that an ethnic or racial group that dominates the upper echelons of a military force may occasionally admit members of other ethnic groups.

Indonesia provides another example of a modern military that is built upon, and to some extent weakened by, ethnic divisions. During the colonial period the Dutch deliberately organized the military along ethnic lines, just as they did the Indonesian labor force and civil service. The war of independence in the 1940s, although serving as the basis of modern-day Indonesian nationalism, also accentuated ethnic divisions within the military. Today, four decades later, military men from the ethnic Javanese community dominate Indonesia's government. Some non-Javanese men have risen to the rank of general, but as those exceptional individuals climbed the military ladder, they tended to cement their ties with the Javanese, often by marrying Javanese women.[10] The Indonesian experience suggests that an ethnic or racial group that dominates the upper echelons of a military force may occasionally admit members of other ethnic groups, but usually only if those members of other groups show that their ties to their own ethnic communities are weak.

In Indonesia as in other Southeast Asian countries, military forces are rapidly expanding their influence on public policy and the economy by acquiring advanced weaponry and political leverage. (Much of that politically significant weaponry comes from foreign allies, including the United States.)

At the same time, however, those forces remain ethnically skewed and ethnically sensitive. This

142

does not mean that they are commanded by officials who read the latest census reports at breakfast and then redeploy divisions and redesign recruiting brochures on the basis of the morning's calculations. But it does suggest that talking simply about the "Malaysian military" or the "Philippine military" is naive. Each force reflects the current ethnic disparities in its country. And as each of these military institutions expands its influence, the political disparities among ethnic groups are, in turn, accentuated (as was the case especially in the Philippines under Marcos's rule).[11]

The Myths of Building a Nation by Rebuilding a Military

The experiences of new or reorganized nations thus reveal the fallacies of two important, related myths about the political usefulness of the military. The first is that military service brings diverse ethnic groups together into a unified nation; the second is that the existence of an effective fighting force signifies the integrity of the political unit it represents. Together these myths foster the idea that once members of a society's diverse groups can be brought together into a military force, the people of the society will view themselves as members of a unified nation. Participation in the military is portrayed as a galvanizing experience for young men and a symbol of the full inclusion of their respective ethnic groups within the power structure of the society. The ranks in which most minority personnel are placed and their distribution within the different branches are rarely seen as relevant aspects of this picture. Events in Lebanon and Kenya, however, demonstrate the fallacy of the two myths and the danger of ignoring the distribution of minority personnel within the ranks of the military.

The first myth is that military service brings diverse ethnic groups together into a unified nation; the second is that the existence of an effective fighting force signifies the integrity of the political unit it represents.

In the summer of 1982, the area of the world perhaps most shaped by ethnic relationships within the military was the Middle East. Israel's deep military incursion into Lebanon, the PLO's military resistance in and subsequent exodus from West Beirut, and the continuing presence of the Syrian

Participation in the military is portrayed as a galvanizing experience for young men and a symbol of the full inclusion of their respective ethnic groups within the power structure of the society.

force all accentuated the weakness of Lebanon as a nation. That weakness was thrown into sharp relief by the ineffectiveness of the Lebanese military. In order not to be simply everyone else's battlefield, diplomats reasoned, Lebanon somehow had to construct its own viable military. Rebuilding the Lebanese military was being touted as the sine qua non not only of a Lebanese peace but also of a general peace throughout the Middle East.

Yet, the Lebanese military is itself the product of inter-ethnic hostilities that came to a head during the 1975-76 civil war and virtually dismembered the army and the air force. Before the civil war, the military command was dominated by Maronite Christians, while a sizeable portion of the rank and file was Lebanese Muslim. Today, despite the commitment of the coalition government to reforming the military so that it inspires the trust of all sectors of the local populace, the officer corps remains dominated by Christians.[12] What has changed as a result of the escalating violence of the past decade is that men of the different Lebanese communities find it even more difficult than before to trust each other; and at the same time, an entire generation of Lebanese young men has been raised to think that bearing weapons outside the confines of the state's military is the sign of being a "real man" and a communal loyalist. Thus, although the army includes only 23,000-26,000 men, it is not the smallness of their numbers but their ethnic divisions that make them ineffective.[13]

Moreover, since 1975 virtually every ethnic or religious community in Lebanon has formed its own militia. Some of them are aided by the Israeli military, others by the PLO military, and still others by the Syrian military (which had 15,000 troops in Lebanon in July 1982).[14] The Israeli and Syrian militaries themselves are ethnically unrepresentative. Israel's military excludes Israeli Arabs, who constitute 14 percent of Israel's population, and Syria's military is commanded by members of the Alawite Sunni Muslim minority.

After a traumatic civil war like Lebanon's or in the wake of a mutiny or a coup attempt, there is

always talk of reforming or even rebuilding the
military to ensure that such an illegal move is not
repeated and to replace those who are indicted for
illegal action. The Kenyan military, though far from
being a shambles like the Lebanese military, was
facing such a situation in the summer of 1982.

Members of the Kenyan air force, charging senior
politicians with corruption and mismanagement, had
attempted to overthrow the regime headed by President Daniel arap Moi. The coup leaders' charges
notwithstanding, it is very likely that ethnic rivalries
played a role both in the attempt and its foiling.

Kenya's independence leader and first president,
Jomo Kenyatta, was a member of the country's
largest ethnic group, the Kikuyu. The air force had
been created after independence from Britain; and of
all the branches of the Kenyan military, the air force
was the most Kikuyu in its ethnic makeup. President
arap Moi, on the other hand, is a member of the Luo,
one of Kenya's smallest ethnic groups.

The coup failed, largely because the police and
key army units refused to support it. Those organizations had histories of being manned by members of
other ethnic groups that the British colonial rulers
trusted more than they trusted the Kikuyu. A month
after the foiled coup, President arap Moi disbanded
the 2,100-man air force. It was later reconstituted
with men considered more loyal to Moi.

To fully under this episode, one has to take into
account the way in which long-standing ethnic
rivalries may spill over into contemporary political
and military institutions. The potential effects of
external factors, including the effects of foreign aid,
also have to be considered. For example, political
leaders can use aid from the United States, and other
countries can be used to enhance or diminish the
relative influence of various ethnic groups.[15]

*The notion that
military forces are
peculiarly suited to
help build a "nation,"
and the false assump-
tions behind such an
idea, should be famil-
iar to most Americans.*

The notion that military forces are peculiarly
suited to help build a "nation," and the false assump-
tions behind such an idea, should be familiar to most
Americans, whether or not they have read about
Lebanon's trauma or Kenya's attempted coup.
Blacks, Native Americans, Hispanics, Japanese-

Americans, Irish-Americans, and Americans from Eastern Europe have all been used by the U.S. government in distinctive ways within the military during the past two centuries. Each group has been used in ways that have not always served either its own communal interests or the goal of a racially or ethnically harmonious military.

Manpower Formulas and Ethnic or Racial Insurgency

The unrepresentative character of a government's military can be a message to excluded groups (or groups kept in lower ranks) that they have no place in the political life of that country as that political life is currently constituted. When the disaffected groups try to protest the unfairness of the system, a fearful government often attacks them with military units and militarized police units whose ethnic composition reflects precisely the grievances being protested. This can set into motion a dangerous spiral. Ironically, as the insecure government elite uses more and more force against the dissidents, it is likely to run short of men from the ethnic groups it trusts most. So, as coercion and violence increase, the government finds itself responding by trying to draw recruits first from foreign mercenary sources and then from the very ethnic or racial groups it is charging with insurgency. This is what happened in white-run Rhodesia until that regime collapsed under the strain of untenable contradictions.[16] It is also what has been happening in South Africa.

The unrepresentative character of a government's military can be a message to excluded groups (or groups kept in lower ranks) that they have no place in the political life of that country as that political life is currently constituted.

The Afrikaner civilian elite that governs South Africa today through its Nationalist party has depended not only on support from the English-speaking whites who run the country's major banking, mining, and manufacturing firms, but also on continuing investments from foreign multinational corporations and banks. Increasingly in the 1980s, however, Afrikaner elites are relying on expanded military and police forces to ensure the survival of apartheid-based minority white rule—and all the key

146

security forces are commanded by Afrikaners. Afrikaners also constitute the majority of officers in the air force, navy, and army. South Africa's English-speaking whites have been least prominent in the army and most prominent in the navy, though even that may be changing as the navy gains more prominence in the government's foreign security formulas.[17]

This Afrikaner ethnic strategy has run into severe limitations in the 1980s, however. Until recently, Afrikaner leaders insisted that the South African military not be dependent on the non-white communities for its troops. But to remain independent of those communities, South African officials had to tolerate an ever-increasing drain on the white civilian labor force, since more white men had to be conscripted for longer periods. In the spring of 1982, the government announced that a new conscription and reserve system was to be instituted whereby every white male youth, on leaving school or the university, would serve 720 days of military duty over a period of 12 years. Furthermore, all white men up to the age of 60 who had not been drafted earlier would now be liable for a call-up of 30 days of basic training and 12 days a year of service in local commando units.[18] But those extensions of white male service have not fulfilled the growing demands for manpower dictated by Pretoria's national security strategy.

In the late 1970s, the South African military even began to recruit non-white men as volunteers into their forces. First to be recruited were men from the group that the South African whites had always tried to co-opt, the so-called mixed or coloured community. Soon afterward, the South African government formed an Indian Corps, appealing to Indian community leaders to see this as a new opportunity for advancement and responsibility in a system still ruled by whites. Finally, and with the greatest hesitancy, the Afrikaner-led military began recruiting South African blacks. Black recruits are not confined to unarmed functions such as driving and cooking but are trained for combat roles. Initially, they were deployed primarily in Namibia, where South West Africa People's Organization (SWAPO) guerrillas

To remain independent of [non-white] communities, South African officials had to tolerate an ever-increasing drain on the white civilian labor force, since more white men had to be conscripted for longer periods.

were stepping up their efforts to secure Namibia's independence from South Africa.

In addition, a report by an American anthropologist details how the South African military is deliberately recruiting black soldiers from a Namibian minority ethnic group referred to as Bushmen, or San.[19] According to the report, the South African government claims that Bushmen have long been antagonistic to groups within the SWAPO forces and that the South African military is doing nothing more than providing a vehicle for the Bushmen to act on their sense of anxiety about SWAPO's political ascendancy. The report cites evidence, however, that both the South African government and its ally, the Dutch Reformed Church, have worked together to alienate the Bushmen from other African groups in Namibia and thus to create a potential pool of military recruits.

In the 1970s, according to the report, the South African government began to see the threats to its "internal" security and the threats to its "external" security as essentially the same. Simultaneously, its manpower planners were forecasting a severe shortage of white young men. It was at this juncture that the South African military started systematically recruiting Bushmen as military trackers in Namibia. Tracking was the role to which Bushmen were relegated because white officials believed that tracking was a "natural" skill of this African ethnic group. By 1982, Bushmen were being used for more direct combat roles, a fact that has heightened pre-existing distrust between Bushmen and the ethnic groups supporting SWAPO. The South African army has established its own Ethnological Section, whose officials claim that the military is "civilizing" the Bushmen and protecting their ethnic identity against the more urban cultures of Namibian society.

Thus, the South African white regime is moving inch by inch toward recruiting from the groups it trusts least and whose young men, in fact, have the least reason to risk their lives for the sake of maintaining the status quo. In the process, the white government is being strained by ever more acute contradictions.

The South African government began to see the threats to its "internal" security and the threats to its "external" security as essentially the same. Simultaneously, its manpower planners were forecasting a severe shortage of white young men.

148

Women, Ethnicity, and Military Manpower

When governing officials think about ethnicity, race, and the sorts of soldiers they need, they usually talk in terms of sweeping group stereotypes, such as "martial race." But in fact they think only about the *men* of those groups and of their own ethnic and racial groups. Military forces, it is true, are overwhelmingly "manned" by men. But even in their exclusively male forms, military manpower formulas depend on women in several different ways. And often the very limitations in how male officials understand or view the women in ethnic groups allow those officials to use women militarily when they do not trust the women's sons and husbands.

Governments at different points in their histories become preoccupied with census figures and demographic trends because they are trying to calculate not only today's ethnic canvas but tomorrow's as well. That means they are trying to predict and control the behavior of women as childbearers. And as the officials begin to worry about whether some women have "too few" children and others "too many," they manufacture racial and ethnic stereotypes about women.

When officials have become nervous over declining birth rates and the strain these impose on military recruiters, governments have quite deliberately had policies of promoting "motherhood" as a patriotic duty. The governments of Britain, Germany, the United States, France, the Soviet Union, and all of Eastern Europe have had, or now have, such "motherhood" policies directed at women and couched in terms of national security. How many children should a woman decide to have? How much access should women have to those resources that will allow them to choose when and how many children to have? Often these questions are looked on as matters of military significance, a policy realm in which women have minimal influence.[20]

When national security officials begin to convert their worries about birth-rate trends into strategies for intervening to alter those trends, they rarely act with

When officials have become nervous over declining birth rates and the strain these impose on military recruiters, governments have quite deliberately had policies of promoting "motherhood" as a patriotic duty.

ethnic blinders on. The government would like women from some groups to have more children and women from other groups to have fewer. For instance, the current Soviet government is urging ethnic Russian, but not Asian Soviet, women to have more children.[21] Similarly, in South Africa today white officials are encouraging white women to have more children for the sake of national security but are trying to discourage African women from having large families.[22]

Women are of military concern not just as mothers but as potential military personnel. So often has this fact been erased from military histories that we are only beginning to understand how and when women have been recruited, from which groups, and with what consequences. When male recruits run short, when wars are prolonged, or when casualties have mounted because of particular modes of warfare—these are the circumstances in which commanders are most likely to consider systematically recruiting women into the military.

Not coincidentally, these are also the junctures in military politics when a government faces the prospect of having to recruit men from ethnic groups that have in the past been excluded from the military or kept in the most peripheral military roles. Consequently, women from certain ethnic groups may be recruited into the military when "ethnically preferred" men run short. In 1982 the South African government, known to be very conservative on questions of the home-bound roles of white women, began to enlist white women into the military for the first time. Although the government stopped short of conscripting white women as it conscripts white men, this was a radical departure for the Nationalist party regime. The change is not attributable to Pretoria's having suddenly become sensitive to a South African women's liberation movement. Rather, the change was made because the white men who make South Africa's security policy are desperately short of the white male recruits needed to sustain an apartheid system in the 1980s.

Thus, any discussion of women in the military—a topic that has become popular in the context of

When national security officials begin to convert their worries about birth-rate trends into strategies for intervening to alter those trends, they rarely act with ethnic blinders on.

150

equal rights debates—must include the ethnic and racial context in which women are excluded from, actively recruited into, or actively demobilized from the military.

The ethnic composition of women in the U.S. military changed rapidly during the same period (1972-81) in which the number of military women as a whole grew. The U.S. Department of Defense has reported that by December 1981, black women (who were allowed very little access to the military until World War II) constituted *42 percent* of all women in the enlisted ranks of the U.S. army. (Black women are only 11 percent of the women in the American population as a whole.) This astoundingly high proportion represents a major change from the military of the 1950s and 1960s. Perhaps it can be accounted for partly by black women's lack of economic and educational alternatives in American society of the 1980s. But the figure of 42 percent may also be due to the changing attitudes that military manpower officials have about women, about black men, and about white men as military recruits. In addition, it may be that some U.S. military officials or certain personnel planners are nervous about the rising numbers of black men in the post-draft army but somehow see black women not as blacks but simply as women—both a new resource and a new worry, but without racial differences playing much of a role.

Often the very limitations in how male officials understand or view the women in ethnic groups allow those officials to use women militarily when they do not trust the women's sons and husbands.

A third area in which sex is relevant to the military's ethnic manpower policies is the area of military-related industrial labor. Any government that is drawing more and more men into its military for the sake of fulfilling national security needs necessarily weakens the civilian labor market (unless there is high civilian unemployment and thus a labor surplus). Women are often called upon by the government to fill the holes left in the labor market. This, of course, happens primarily in wartime, and women mobilized to serve in the war industries are usually told they will be needed only "for the duration." Once the war ends, women are expected to give up their newly won, high-paying industrial jobs and return to jobs as unpaid housewives or poorly paid service workers to make way for demobilized male soldiers. And just as women from different ethnic or racial groups do not get the same wartime job opportunities, so they do not face identical pressures to give up their jobs once the military no longer needs their civilian labor. These differences are made graphically clear by the three black and two white women who tell their stories in the celebrated documentary film *The Life and Times of Rosie the Riveter.*

Minority Groups and Manpower Strategies

As different as men's and women's relationships to the military may be, members of both sexes among minority ethnic and racial groups have a stake in bringing out into the open a government's manpower strategies and the consequences of those strategies. Past and present experiences in various countries suggest that most ethnic groups at certain points in their own development lose, or attempt to overcome, their own passivity vis-a-vis the military. Sometimes a particular ethnic group will attempt to overcome its passivity in a fragmented way. It may not articulate its views through organized political parties or well-known spokespersons for the community. Or its reactions may look like diffuse alienation from the military or uncritical respect for it. Or the people picked by the mainstream media or by government agencies to "represent" the entire community may in fact speak only for the men or only for one class within that community. Especially in these latter cases, one should gauge the response of an ethnic group to the military by looking beyond what the "leaders" of the group say. What warnings do mothers give their sons and daughters about the military? What do fathers tell about their military experiences? Do they speak with pride, or embarrassment, or regret? What do young people within the group tell one another?

Members of both sexes among minority ethnic and racial groups have a stake in bringing out into the open a government's manpower strategies and the consequences of those strategies.

At other times, an ethnic group will formulate a more coherent, organized, and articulate position on military manpower and the group's collective relationship to it. Within NATO today, for example, both

152

the Belgian and the Canadian forces are affected by the new sense of political activism among the two countries' less influential ethnic groups. The French Canadians see the military as one of the many federal institutions that have discriminated against them, and during Pierre Trudeau's regime, electoral pressure from the militant French Canadian nationalists compelled the Canadian military to undertake a deliberate campaign to recruit more French Canadians into the officer corps. Similarly in Belgium, the Flemish community has challenged the political and economic dominance of the Walloons, raising questions about the respective roles of the two groups in the Belgian military.

The military is not simply another type of employer. Military forces are major wielders of state power, and groups that are excluded from military policy-making posts have little influence over an enormous portion of public expenditures. The fact that a community has many of its members in the infantry or the nursing corps is no guarantee at all that that community will have any say over military policy. Furthermore, as military forces become more technologically sophisticated, they are seen as "schools" for labor in the most advanced sectors of the society. Groups that have less opportunity to receive military training will have a more difficult time competing in the civilian labor market. Finally, the military is an instrument for maintaining the social structure in ways that serve some interests more than others.

Ethnic groups whose participation in the military is primarily at the rank-and-file level are not likely to have much impact in either altering or sustaining the current social order. As officers, however, members of minority ethnic groups may come to wield some influence. The promotion of minority individuals to officer status is therefore an important step. But only when minority men and women, both inside and outside the military, begin to analyze their own relationships to the military will they be likely to develop a community stance on questions of defense policy and international affairs. Such a stance is a necessary prerequisite of real influence within the military and within the society as a whole.

> *The military is not simply another type of employer. Military forces are major wielders of state power, and groups that are excluded from military policy-making posts have little influence over an enormous portion of public expenditures.*

Endnotes

1. *New York Times,* May 13, 1982.

2. I have explored numerous cases of ethnic-military manpower politics in several recent volumes: see my *Ethnic Soldiers* (Harmondsworth, Eng.: Penguin Books, 1980; Athens, Ga.: University of Georgia Press, 1980), and *Police, Military and Ethnicity: Foundations of State Power* (New Brunswick, N.J.: Transaction Books, 1980). See also Dewitt C. Ellinwood and Cynthia Enloe, eds., *Ethnicity and the Military in Asia* (New Brunswick, N.J.: Transaction Books, 1981).

3. See, for instance, the evolution of the Roman army as described in Michael Grant, *The Army of the Caesars* (New York: Scribners, 1974).

4. Thomas E. Weil et al., *Area Handbook for Peru* (Washington, D.C.: GPO, 1970), and Abraham Lowenthal, ed., *The Peruvian Experiment: Continuity and Change Under Military Rule* (Princeton: Princeton University Press, 1975).

5. Philip Mason, *A Matter of Honor: An Account of the Indian Army, Its Officers and Men* (London: Jonathan Cape, 1974); on the English ideological construction of the Scots as a "martial race," see John Prebble, *Mutiny* (London: Secker and Warburg, 1975).

6. Of related interest is Constance M. Wilson, "Burmese-Karen Warfare 1840-1950: A Thai View," in Ellinwood and Enloe, *Ethnicity and the Military,* pp. 18-52. For descriptions of other monarchical militaries that practiced forced conscription from groups that government did not trust, see Daniel Pipes, *Slave Soldiers and Islam* (New Haven: Yale University Press, 1981).

7. For further western analyses of Soviet ethnic politics, especially as they relate to military affairs, see Michael Rywkin, "Central Asia and Soviet Manpower," *Problems of Communism* 28 ((January-February 1979); Jeremy Azrael, *Emergent Nationalist Problems in the USSR* (Santa Monica: Rand Corporation, 1977); Teresa Rakowska-Harmstone, "The Red

Army as the Instrument of National Integration," paper presented at the Air University Conference on the Role of the Military in Communist Societies, Maxwell Air Force Base, Alabama, November 21-23, 1975; and Joel Moses, "The Politics of Female Labor in the Soviet Union" (Ithaca, N.Y.: Western Societies Program, Occasional Papers, Cornell University, 1978).

8. One analysis that concludes that the Soviet army has succeeded in overcoming ethnic conflict is Ellen Jones and Fred W. Grupp, "Political Socialization in the Soviet Military," *Armed Forces and Society* 18:3 (Spring 1982): 377. For an alternative analysis, see Helene Carrere d'Encausse, *Decline of an Empire: The Soviet Socialist Republics in Revolt* (New York: Harper Colophon, 1981).

9. Les Aspin, "The Soviet Soldier," *New York Times,* June 8, 1982; and d'Encausse, *Decline of an Empire,* pp. 161-164.

10. Ann Gregory, "The Influence of Ethnicity in the Evolution of the Indonesian Military Elite," in Ellinwood and Enloe, *Ethnicity and the Military,* pp. 267-295.

11. On the Philippines, see Enloe, *Ethnic Soldiers,* pp. 177-179, 204-206; on Malaysia, see Zakaria Haji Ahmad, "The Bayonet and the Truncheon: Army-Police Relations in Malaysia," in Ellinwood and Enloe, *Ethnicity and the Military,* pp. 67-92.

12. William E. Farrell, "Lebanon's Army May Get Peacekeeping Role in Beirut," *New York Times,* June 22, 1982, Section A, p. 8.

13. Ibid.

14. Ibid; Thomas Friedman, "At Bay", Week In Review Desk, *New York Times,* July 4, 1982, Section 4, p.1.

15. Alan Cowell, "Leader of Kenyan Coup Attempt Said To Have Been A Private", *New York Times,* August 29, 1982, Section 1, p. 20; "Kenya Disbands Its Air Force After Coup Bid", *New York Times,* August 22, 1982, Section 1, p. 12.

16. Cynthia Enloe, "Mercenarization," in Western Massachusetts Concerned African Scholars, *U.S.*

Military Involvement in South Africa (Boston: South End Press, 1978); Enloe, *Ethnic Soldiers,* pp. 78-82.

17. Enloe, "Ethnic Factors in the Evolution of the South African Military," *Police, Military and Ethnicity.*

18. "South Africa: The 20 Percent Gets All the Effort," *The Economist,* April 3, 1982, p. 72.

19. Robert Gordon, "Namibia: South Africa's Pact with the Bushmen," *Anthropology Resource Center Newsletter* 6 (March 1982): 6

20. Studies that detail the U.S. government's policies toward motherhood in the context of national security include Karen Anderson, *Wartime Women: Sex Roles, Family Relations, and the Status of Women during World War II* (Westport, Conn., and London: Greenwood Press, 1981); Marion Frank, Marily Ziebarth, and Connie Field, *The Life and Times of Rosie the Riveter* (Emeryville, Calif.: Clarity Educational Productions, 1982); Carol B. Berkin and Clara M. Lovett, *Women, War, and Revolution* (New York: Holmes and Meier, 1980); Susan Hartmann, *The Home Front and Beyond: American Women in the 1940s* (Boston: Twayne Publishers, 1982); and Leila Rupp, *Mobilizing Women for War: German and American Propaganda, 1939-45* (Princeton: Princeton University Press, 1978).

21. Joel Moses, "Politics of Female Labor" and "Birth Rate Politics in Eastern Europe and the USSR," *ISIS: International Bulletin,* no. 7 (Spring 1978), pp. 26-28; and D'Encausse, *Decline of an Empire,* pp. 77-82.

22. "Intelligence: Reproduce!" *Parade Magazine,* March 18, 1979; and United Nations Centre against Apartheid, "The Effects of Apartheid on the Status of Women in South Africa," *Notes and Documents,* no. 7/8, May 1978.

11. RIGHT ISSUES, WRONG QUESTIONS

Roger Wilkins

The problem conjured up under the heading "Blacks in the Military" demonstrates about as clearly as anything can the perverse ways in which racism blinds powerful American individuals and institutions not only to the needs of millions of this country's citizens, but also to the basic long-term interests of the society.

The starting point of any consideration of these issues has to be the life conditions faced by lower income blacks—the group from which the military draws most heavily. Few would dissent from the propositions that people in that group face great difficulties in their lives and that the blows they receive as they are growing up and being shaped are particularly devastating. However, the standard arguments about such people treat them as abstractions who are either innately inferior or whose lives demonstrate the failures and unfairness of the American system. In such discussions, the consequences to the individuals or to America in general of systematically inflicting massive injury on broad classes of people are rarely faced, except theoretically. The mechanism of denial—a central element of racism—often blunts careful consideration of the damage done to individuals.

But when blacks go into the military in significant numbers, important people who otherwise would spend little time worrying about them as individuals immediately show concern about what has been done to them, what can be made of them, and whether or not the injuries inflicted on them by poverty, inferior education, a terrible environment, and harsh rejection can be repaired sufficiently for them to serve America effectively.

When blacks go into the military in significant numbers, important people who otherwise would spend little time worrying about them as individuals immediately show concern about what has been done to them.

157

Thinking constructively about lower income blacks does not come naturally to most of the people who think about military issues, however, so it is difficult for them to frame the right questions even when they are finally focusing on just the right issues. Thus, instead of asking the logical national security question—what must we change in our society to ensure a continuous flow of able enlistees for our armed services?—they generally ask questions whose purpose is to measure the extent to which the injured people will damage the ideal of military readiness. Will the military be smart enough? Will it be effective? Will it be reliable in political and other senses? Do Europeans want an army containing so many black people stationed in their countries even if it is supposed to be protecting them?

The black response is somewhat different and is a natural result of the rough conditioning blacks get in America. Blacks look at how black enlistments and reenlistments have swollen in the last decade. They hear experts say that blacks would constitute 30 percent of the casualties in the next conventional war. And these figures make them ask themselves: is it fair?

*I*nstead of asking the logical national security question—what must we change in our society to ensure a continuous flow of able enlistees for our armed services?—they generally ask questions whose purpose is to measure the extent to which the injured people will damage the ideal of military readiness.

The numbers do tend to command attention. Although only 13 percent of America's youth population is black, some 20 percent of active-duty enlisted personnel are black, and so are about 30 percent of enlisted men in the army. Since 1970, the percentage of blacks in the military has nearly doubled. Much of the increase has been attributed to the fact that the United States gave up conscription and adopted the all-volunteer force in January 1973.

Considering the almost unbearable clumsiness with which so many white people deal with racial issues in the United States, it is not surprising that questions based on the percentages of blacks in the military have elicited a great deal of attention. For example, in an article published in the U.S. Civil Rights Commission quarterly, *Perspectives* (Spring 1982), Jeremy Feigelson quoted General David Jones, then chairman of the Joint Chiefs of Staff, who said during congressional testimony:

> I am deeply concerned that, without a broad commitment to a national cross section in

uniform, economic and demographic pressures could produce a "volunteer" armed force peopled by economic conscripts—and one without the discipline, attitudes, or cohesiveness needed for a modern global strategy.

Lawrence Korb in chapter 3 sums up the objections to the all-volunteer force succinctly: "The all-volunteer force has been subjected to a number of criticisms—that it is too black, too female, too dumb, too small, too expensive, and has too few reserves." When describing the concerns of the people who have the greatest professional interest in our military—officials in the Defense Department, our allies, and our adversaries—he indicates that the priorities narrow: "What they want to know is, 'Can they fight?'"

Since Korb is very knowledgeable about the quality of the American military and has a direct interest in the issue, it is worth lingering a moment over his observations. In fact, they might give some comfort to the people for whom racial stereotypes cause anxiety about the makeup of the armed forces. He says, for example, that there has been a recent downward trend in the percentage of black enlistees. A similar point, made by Charles Moskos in chapter 7, is that in recent years the percentage of blacks enlisting after earning high school diplomas has exceeded the percentage of whites enlisting with that amount of education. And if the normal stereotyped linkage between blacks and stupidity retains its vitality, then Korb's report that the number of enlistees in the lowest allowable aptitude category— category IV—is dramatically decreasing should also ease racist fears. Whereas the percentage of enlistees in that category in 1980 was 50 percent of all enlistees, by 1982 it had declined to 18 percent. Korb also notes that approximately 80 percent of the people taken into the military are high school graduates and that the aptitude or "trainability" scores of the enlistees are slightly higher than those of the society at large. "Generally," he said, "the all-volunteer force is fairly representative of the civilian society on all demographic characteristics except race and sex."

Korb draws two fundamental conclusions. The first is that the all-volunteer force can be made to

If the normal stereotyped linkage between blacks and stupidity retains its vitality, then Korb's report that the number of enlistees in the lowest allowable aptitude category— category IV—is dramatically decreasing should also ease racist fears.

work if we do three things: we must maintain a competitive pay scale; we must keep the force ready by supplying the military with the equipment it needs and by giving it the respect of the American people; and we must face honestly such questions as the proper military roles of women and blacks. His second conclusion is that all the solutions offered by the critics of the all-volunteer force raise more questions than they answer.

Since the military is both darker and poorer than the population as a whole, the service is deemed unrepresentative. But in another sense, the military is quite representative. It accurately reflects the nation's power relationships and its social and economic problems.

Even allowing for the fact that an assistant secretary of defense can hardly be expected to announce in a public forum that the United States has put together a military that is too black and too dumb to be of any great utility in wartime, Korb's arguments on behalf of the course on which the military is currently embarked seem both measured and reasonable. The military seems to be working hard to ensure that its people are both trainable and well trained. Korb has given the impression that the armed services are making serious efforts to distribute both the risks and the opportunities of military service equitably. He reports, for example, that the percentage of blacks entering combat arms has been decreasing in recent years and that strenuous efforts are being made to enrich the occupational opportunities available to black enlistees. Thus, whatever concerns others may have, his report should be reassuring to those who have a balanced concern about the efficacy of an all-volunteer force, to those who believe that lower income blacks are both inept and inferior, and to those who hope that blacks, once inside the military, can find some measure of equity.

But not everyone finds the official presentations of the Pentagon persuasive. Apparently, many in Congress are deeply concerned about the substantial number of blacks in the military. Some view conscription as the answer to the problem of representation, and they also believe that conscription would make the military cheaper to maintain. Korb has indicated that in Europe, as well, there is a problem. Officials of our NATO allies have informally expressed their concern that our military sends "too many blacks" to their countries. They, too, would like to see the United States reinstitute conscription.

Korb and Representative Les Aspin of Wisconsin (chapter 4) argue forcefully that conscription would

160

create more problems than it would solve. They point out that, whereas the draft was an almost universal experience for young men during World War II and in the 1950s, the military's current manpower needs would require service by a smaller percentage of the current youth population. Those pressed into service would therefore see themselves as having been unfairly selected to bear a burden that was not equitably shared throughout society. Moreover, to make the military cheaper, the conscripts would have to be paid a substantially lower wage than volunteers are currently earning. Thus, those required to serve would be doubly damned, since most of their peers would be avoiding service and those serving would be poorly compensated. Considering these problems of unfairness, Aspin and others oppose the reintroduction of conscription because they believe it to be politically untenable.

Some of us have proved unwilling to abandon so easily an extension of that idea—that there would be positive value in requiring virtually all young Americans to render some form of service to the country. We have argued that universal national service, which would include military service, would eliminate both levels of unfairness. The experience of serving the nation would be shared by almost everyone, and all would receive minimal compensation. Such a program would be valuable, we argue, because it would instill a sense of community in young Americans who might otherwise be exposed only to lessons that teach individualism at the expense of community. Although expressing sympathy for those arguments, Representative Aspin has seemed quite convinced that such a program would be too expensive for the country to bear and impossible for the government to run efficiently.

If America cannot provide enough jobs for the black youth population, a good part of that population will show up in the armed services.

Charles Moskos levels another charge at the all-volunteer force. He describes it as being staffed according to market principles in ways that injure not only blacks but also the concept of American democracy in general. His objection is that the all-volunteer market mechanism has produced a military force composed of recruits from the lower class of both blacks and whites. That situation raises the fundamental issue of whether or not it can possibly be deemed good public policy to expect lower income youths to stand ready, and perhaps to fight, to preserve a society in which the most cherished privileges are largely denied them. In considering that problem, we should note that it is apparently not peculiar to the all-volunteer force. Korb's observation that even during conscription the army tended to recruit the "leftovers" suggests that the issues raised in this context go beyond current recruiting methods and the reliability of the armed services to fundamental long-term issues of how burdens, opportunities, and rewards are distributed in this society.

Moskos suggests that we might lessen the impact of market principles on the composition of the services by shaping a package of incentives for service that is so inviting that many middle-class youngsters will enlist. That might indeed inject more class balance into the military force structure. For lower-class black youths, however, it merely shifts the question from whether it is fair for many of them to have no economic option but military service to whether it is fair that some of them lose the valuable economic option of military service so that we can entice more middle-class youngsters into the military.

In the Pentagon, at least, attention must therefore be paid to problems that are minimized or ignored in private life. So long as the nation does not care enough to educate poor black youngsters well, those educational disabilities will show up in military aptitude test scores and the Pentagon will be forced to pay attention.

The Moskos solution leads to a basic truth about the problem of blacks in the military. Like Moskos, other people worry about the problem of representation in the armed services (whether for reasons that I would laud or for reasons that I would decry). And like him, most of those people focus on whether or not the color and the class structure inside the military constitute a rough representation of the nation's youth population as a whole. Since the military is both darker and poorer than the population as a whole, the service is deemed unrepresentative. But in another sense, the military is quite representative. It accurately reflects the nation's power relationships and its social and economic problems. If America cannot provide enough jobs for the black youth population, a good part of that population will show up in the armed services.

In the Pentagon, at least, attention must therefore be paid to problems that are minimized or ignored in private life. So long as the nation does not care enough to educate poor black youngsters well, those educational disabilities will show up in military aptitude test scores and the Pentagon will be forced to pay attention. If the logic of market principles dictates that our military be manned by the children of the poor, then a number of people of conscience in the society will also pay attention.

If, however, we try to ameliorate the social and economic problems that reveal themselves in our military by broadening the demographic representation within the ranks, many blacks who would have escaped the problems of America by enlisting are forced again to become victims of the very problems that caused the imbalances in the military in the first place. The problem, therefore, would not be solved, but simply shifted back onto the shoulders of poor, black, undereducated individuals. Solving the problems of the military will thus leave untouched the troubles in the nation as a whole, which can be solved only if profound racial and economic adjustments are made in American society.

It is in that context that one must consider the poignant ethical question about black overrepresentation: is it fair? Congressman John Cavanaugh, as quoted by Robert K. Fullinwider (chapter 8), put the negative case most vividly:

> The fatal defect in the all-volunteer force is that . . . it is not a "volunteer" system at all. The AVF has proven an unjust and inequitable system of economic and racial conscription. A system in which those who have the least in our society are offered the opportunity to be trained to risk all in exchange for the very thing they have been denied by the society they are asked to defend, a job.

Fullinwider, though, makes a powerful case for the proposition that under current circumstances—in a nation at peace that pays its enlistees an amount thought equivalent to the salary of unskilled entry-level workers in the private sector—the choice confronting minority youths is not, on the face of it, unfair. Even if one is not fully persuaded by Fullinwider's argument, it would be hard to dispute that, given current economic and racial conditions in America, the situation facing young blacks today is far less unfair than it would be if there were no

If, however, we try to ameliorate the social and economic problems that reveal themselves in our military by broadening the demographic representation within the ranks, many blacks who would have escaped the problems of America by enlisting are forced again to become victims of the very problems that caused the imbalances in the military in the first place.

163

military option whatsoever available to them. The problem of equity, after all, just like the problems of representation, the capacities of black soldiers, racist anxieties, and political reliability, cannot be removed from what goes on in the larger society. In that light, it appears that the military does a better job of making, enlarging, and sustaining opportunities for minorities than do most other segments of society. For that reason, the military seems to be making better progress in dealing with the problems of readiness than the howls of many critics of the all-volunteer force would indicate.

In the end, the problem of equity and all the other problems that seem to worry people so—readiness, reliability, the reactions of the allies—must await a time when the focus shifts away from the military and toward the society that produced it and that it is supposed to protect.

Despite these successes by the armed forces, criticism of the all-volunteer force persists. Those who care little about gross inequalities of opportunity in this society seem capable of real concern only when the inequalities have an impact on the institutions established to defend that society. They then seek to attend to the problems of the institutions rather than to the problems of the American citizens who—in their view—are weakening the institutions. Dealt with in that fashion, few of the problems will be solved satisfactorily. It may even be that, given current conditions, the problem of equity for blacks is the least troubling of the whole constellation of issues wrapped up under the heading of blacks and the military.

In the end, the problem of equity and all the other problems that seem to worry people so—readiness, reliability, the reactions of the allies—must await a time when the focus shifts away from the military and toward the society that produced it and that it is supposed to protect.